BETWEEN FENCES

This collection of essays serves as the catalog for Between Fences, an exhibition organized by the National Building Museum, Washington, D.C.

This catalog was made possible by a grant from **The Furthermore program of The J.M. Kaplan Fund**. The National Building Museum is grateful for its sponsorship.

The exhibition, on view at the Museum from May 31, 1996 through January 5, 1997, was made possible by:

PATRONS

Allied Tube & Conduit
American Fence Association
Master-Halco, Inc.
Merchants Metals
Sonco Worldwide, Inc.

SPONSORS

American Tube & Pipe Company, Inc.
Ameristar Fence Products
Bekaert Corporation
Boundary Fence & Railing Systems, Inc.
Century Tube Corporation
Hohulin Brothers Fence Company, Ltd.
Ideal Fencing Corporation
Keystone Steel & Wire Company
Qual Line Fence Corporation
Reeves Southeastern Corporation
Western Tube & Conduit Corporation
Wheatland Tube Company

CONTRIBUTORS

Allied Fence Manufacturing Company
American Zinc Association
Anchor Fence, Inc.
Anchor Fence Company of Northeast
    New York, Inc.
Big River Zinc Corporation

Brooklyn Fence Distributors, Inc.
Builders Fence Company, Inc.
California Chapter of the American
    Fence Association
Cargill Steel & Wire
Carolinas Fence Association, Chapter of
    the American Fence Association
Clinton Fence Company
DAC Industries
Garden State Chapter of the American
    Fence Association
Long Fence
NASCO, Inc.
National Wholesale Fence Supply, Inc.
Northeast Chapter of the American
    Fence Association
Page Two, Inc.
Past Presidents' Club of the American
    Fence Association
Robinson Iron Corporation
Security Fence Manufacturing & Supply
    Company, Inc.
South Florida Fence Association, Chapter
    of the American Fence Association
Southwestern Wire, Inc.
USA Industries, Inc.
Wisconsin-Northern Illinois Chapter of
    the American Fence Association
World Fence News
Zinc Corporation of America

The National Building Museum thanks Sonny Long of Sonco Worldwide, Inc. for his leadership in raising funds for the exhibition. In addition, Mark Levin of the Chain Link Fence Manufacturers Institute and Terry Dempsey of the American Fence Association provided essential support.

BETWEEN FENCES

Exhibition organized and catalog
edited by Gregory K. Dreicer

Essays by

Diana Balmori

Estella M. Chung

Philip Dole

Gregory K. Dreicer

John B. Jackson

Gary Kulik

Anne M. Lange

Anne Stillman

National Building Museum, Washington, D.C.
Princeton Architectural Press, New York

Published by
National Building Museum
401 F Street NW
Washington, D.C. 20001

and

Princeton Architectural Press
37 East 7th Street
New York, NY 10003

© 1996 National Building Museum,
all rights reserved

ISBN: 1-56898-080-9
First Edition
00 99 98 97 96   5 4 3 2 1

Library of Congress Cataloging-in-
Publication data for this title available
from the publisher

Printed and bound in the United States

For a free catalog of books published by
Princeton Architectural Press, call toll free:
800. 722. 6657

Curator and Supervising Editor:
Gregory K. Dreicer

Editor: Maggie Kelly

Project Assistant: Estella M. Chung

Book Design:
J. Abbott Miller, Ji Byol Lee
Design/Writing/Research

Exhibition Design: Boym Design Studio

© 1996 National Building Museum
and Princeton Architectural Press

COVER: *Security guard opening gate,*
Buick plant, Melrose Park, Illinois, 1941
Photograph by Ken Hedrich, Hedrich-
Blessing, courtesy Chicago Historical
Society, HB-06781-C.

CONTENTS

FOREWORD

We shape our dwellings, and afterwards our dwellings shape us," Winston Churchill once wrote. Exploring this interplay is the role of the National Building Museum, the only institution in the United States devoted to American achievements in architecture, engineering, planning, construction, and design. We encourage people to consider the cultural, political, and technological forces that mold the built environment and the ways in which the products of building impact our lives.

The Between Fences project is a prime example of this dynamic. Through an exploration of the many fence types that traverse our landscape—enclosing homes, fields, factories, and public buildings—the exhibition and catalog tell a complex story about the colonization and expansion of the United States. They inspire us to use the built world as a means of examining ourselves as individuals, communities, and a nation.

Gregory K. Dreicer, who curated the exhibition and served as editor of this catalog, has done a skillful job of exploring the meaning of the fence in the American landscape. The contributors to this volume also brought their rich backgrounds to bear on the question of why Americans build as they do.

I am grateful to the fence manufacturers and builders who provided us with a fascinating story to tell and who continue to shape the landscape. Their financial support and enthusiastic encouragement have been essential. I would also like to thank the many institutions and individuals who have helped us.

I am particularly grateful to The Furthermore program of The J. M. Kaplan Fund, which made publication of this catalog possible. The generous support of the Kaplan Fund enables us to present our work to a broad public and to continue developing programs that help people understand the built environment, preserve its past, and determine its future.

Susan Henshaw Jones
President and Director
National Building Museum

INTRODUCTION

We live between fences. We may hardly notice them, but they are dominant figures in our lives. Our past is defined by the cutting point of barbed wire and the staccato rhythm of the homey white picket. Fences are essential to the way we think about land, the way we behave on that land, and the way we expect our land to look. They bound our properties and stand at the center of the American landscape.

Fences define, protect, confine, and liberate. They tell us where we belong and who we are in relation to others. Fences join the public and private. Remove a fence; invite chaos. Erect a fence; you are home.

Fences give order to a vast continent. They frame space and encourage people to perceive land as a patchwork of properties. Fences announce who has access to the earth's resources. With a fence, a tract of land becomes a park or parking lot; it becomes mine or yours or ours. Fences make space into place.

Like the computer and telephone systems that link and isolate, fences form a communications network. They help shape community and identity. At the same time, fences protect crops from cattle, they protect others from us, and us from ourselves.

Fences comprise an endless variety of structures and materials. They represent an enormous investment of labor, capital, and creative thought. Fences stand thanks to inventors, manufacturers, construction workers, mechanics, legislators, and homeowners.

This is an introduction to an introduction: *Between Fences* begins a comprehensive exploration of the history and meanings of the fence in North America. Eight essayists view fences of rails, pickets, hedge, and wire. They examine the role of the fence in the settlement of America, discuss America's most widely built fences, look at hedges as historic and contemporary landscape elements, analyze Robert Frost's ambivalence, assess the relationship of barbed wire to changes in the West, and search for the origins of chain link. The exhibition raises questions concerning identity and public and private space, as it looks at the role of boundaries in neighborly, community, and international relations. The bibliograpy at the end of this catalog supplies references to fences of all types, from stone walls to ornamental metal. I hope that *Between Fences* encourages further examination of the relationship between fences and the land in which they stand.

I am indebted to many individuals and companies, many more than can be mentioned in this space. I would like to thank the members of the fence industry whose backing made the *Between Fences* project possible. The generous sponsorship of The Furthermore program of The J.M. Kaplan Fund bolstered our confidence and gave us the wherewithal to create this catalog. Publisher Kevin C. Lippert and designers J. Abbott Miller and Ji Byol Lee were our resourceful partners in its realization. Essential to the entire project was the support of the President and Director of the National Building Museum, Susan Henshaw Jones, Chief Curator Joseph Rosa, and his predecessor Melissa McLoud. The catalog and exhibition could not have been completed without the assistance and dedication of Estella Chung and Betsy May-Salazar. The help, advice, and encouragement of Maggie Kelly were crucial to every aspect of *Between Fences*.

Gregory K. Dreicer
Curator

FENCES AND THE SETTLEMENT OF NEW ENGLAND

Anne Stillman

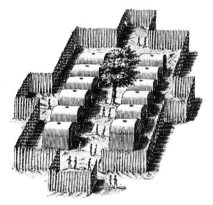

When colonists settled in America during the early seventeenth century, they left behind a land that had been domesticated for centuries and entered what was to them a wilderness fraught with unknown dangers. They proceeded to appropriate and subjugate the land, and one of the most important means they used to do so was the building of fences.

For the early colonists of New England, the fence was a fundamental element of survival. High fences enclosed the earliest settlements and protected them from attack. Of equal importance, fences protected the food supply from being devoured by domestic animals. Fences also became part of a complex legal argument the colonists used to justify their claim to Native American land.

The earliest accounts of fences describe palisades or stockades—fences for fortification of the settlements. English colonists built such defenses both in Virginia and in Massachusetts. In 1610, William Strachey described a palisade around Jamestown made of planks and posts that were anchored in the ground.[1] In Plymouth, a little more than two years after the Mayflower landed, the colonists built a stockade around their settlement. Edward Winslow wrote in 1622/23: "Knowing our own weakness...and still lying open to all casualty, having as yet (under God) no other defense than our arms, we thought it most needful to impale our town: which we accomplished in the month of February, and some few days."[2] This fence impressed John Pory, an Englishman who had spent three

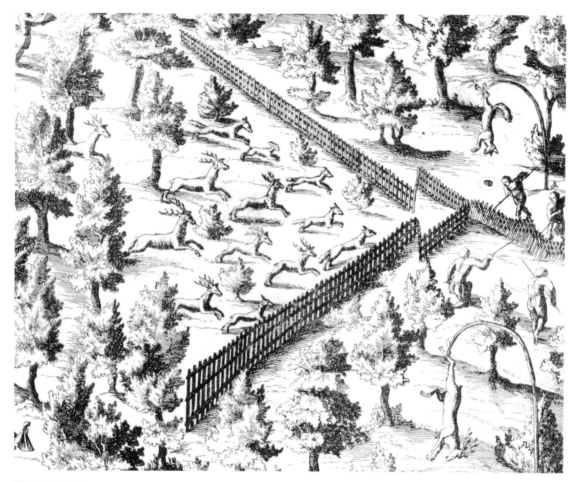

Native Americans
capturing deer and
foxes, 1632

years as an official in Virginia and visited Plymouth in 1622/23. He wrote, "Their industry...appeareth by their building, as by a substantial palisado about their [town] of twenty-seven hundred foot in compass, stronger than I have seen any in Virginia."[3]

Native Americans also built fences for fortification. Surviving engravings and watercolors show stockades built by Native Americans in Florida, the Carolinas, and in the northeast. Miles Standish of Plymouth encountered abandoned Native American fortifications in 1621 on a scouting expedition and wrote, "We came to a fort built in the manner thus: there were poles some thirty or forty feet long, stuck in the ground as thick as they could be set one by another, and with these they enclosed a ring some forty or fifty feet over."[4] The height of this fence must have seemed remarkable to Standish, although it was not reproduced at Plymouth, where the palisade was about eight feet high.[5] Although no contemporaneous pictures of the Plymouth stockade exist, we can visualize fairly well what it looked like, and there is a reconstruction of it at Plimoth Plantation. This type of fence has persisted with little alteration to the present day, though it is now used primarily for privacy rather than protection.

An early seventeenth-century illustration, inspired by the words of the explorer Samuel de Champlain, shows Native Americans in Canada using a fence in a very different manner. Champlain described a V-shaped fence made of eight- or nine-foot stakes placed side by side. Native Americans are shown chasing deer and foxes toward the fence, which is used to corner them while spearmen stand at the ready.[6] In New England, Native Americans sometimes piled up brush and loose timber to construct temporary fences for the same purpose during peak hunting season.[7]

However ingenious this use of fences may have been, it did not constitute "enclosing the land." In the eyes of the colonists, it was the act of enclosing land with a fence that bestowed ownership. John Winthrop, the first governor of the Massachusetts Bay Colony, crafted a justification for the taking of land from the native peoples: "That which lies common, and hath never beene replenished or subdued is free to any that possess and improve it." He went on to explain that "The first right was naturall when men held the earth in common, every man sowing and feeding where he pleased: then as men and theire cattell encreased they appropriated certaine parcells of Grownde by inclosing and peculiar manuerance, and this in time got them a Civill right." Winthrop cited some biblical examples and summed up his position thus: "As for the Natives in New England, they inclose no land, neither have any setled habytation, nor any tame Cattle to improve land by, and soe have no other but a Naturall Right to those Countries, soe as if we leave them sufficient for their use, we may lawfully take the rest, there being more than enough for them and us."[8]

Winthrop's opinion that unenclosed land was the colonists for the taking was adopted as law in the Massachusetts Bay Colony, modified only by the one concession to the Native Americans that cultivation counted as improving the land. The Massachusetts courts therefore acknowledged the Native Americans' right to their unenclosed cornfields, but not to the rest of their territory.

Fences were vital to the colonists, not only as defenses against hostile Native Americans and wild animals, but also as protection for crops. Without fences, crops were subject to depredation by livestock; without crops, famine could ensue. The building and maintenance of fences therefore became a matter for legal regulation in seventeenth-century New England.

Native Americans had no domestic animals except for dogs, so before the arrival of the English, they had neither the tradition nor the need to fence their fields. As the colonists' livestock inevitably got into the unfenced Native American crops, many disputes occurred. Before long, Native Americans had no choice but to adopt the practice of fencing their growing fields to avoid continual damage.

Although there was variation from town to town, the typical land system in early New England was very different from later systems of private property and individual farms. Home lots were grants of smallish parcels varying in size depending on the town, but usually ranging between one and five acres. Each of these contained a house and its outbuildings and probably fenced-in

Territoriality in humans supposes a control over an area or space that must be conceived of and communicated.

Robert David Sack, *Human Territoriality* (1986)

dooryards and barnyards. The home lots were laid out side by side along the streets, and ordinances sometimes required that fences be built to divide one home lot from another.

The planting fields were located beyond the clustered houses and were held in common by the proprietors of the town. Each proprietor was allotted a portion of the field to till for his own use, but decisions such as the date of harvest were arrived at communally. One man often had a share in a few different fields in scattered locations. Pastures were also held in common, and the most valuable animals, such as oxen, horses, and milking cows, were usually attended by a community herdsman during the day and returned to their barnyards at night. Sheep were watched over by town shepherds, and at night the flocks were sometimes protected in moveable pens.

Since labor was scarce, it was more practical to separate the crops from the animals by fencing in the planting fields than by enclosing the large areas needed for pasture. Farmers were assigned a section of the common fence to build or maintain. If anyone failed to make his section of fence secure, the crops of much of the community would be at risk.

Before long, the maintenance of fences became a matter of law. The Connecticut Colony enacted fence legislation in 1643/44, because the "unruliness of some kinde of Cattle" and the "insufficiency of many fences" were causing many differences that could become "very prejuditiall to the publique peace."[9] Officials, known as fence viewers, were appointed by towns throughout New England to survey the condition of fences, usually those enclosing fields. Fence upkeep was so crucial to the welfare of towns, that in Fairfield, Connecticut, four men were appointed as fence viewers in 1677/78, while only two were appointed to survey the condition of the roads.[10] In this early instance of regulation, field fences had to meet standards of durability or be fixed within a set amount of time, usually not more than a few days. If the fences were not repaired quickly enough, fines were levied. Leaving a gate open to a common field was also an infraction subject to penalty.

As a further precaution for the safety of the crops, hogs were pastured miles away from the villages. They were the most troublesome of the colonists' animals, as they often managed to break through fences. Consequently, they were the subject of endless complaints. Hogs that remained near town were eventually required to wear yokes to hamper their ability to wriggle through fence rails.

You may as well think of stopping a crow as those hogs. They will go to a distance from a fence, take a run, and leap through the rails three or four feet from the ground, turning themselves sidewise.

Richard Parkinson, *Tour of America* (1805)

OPPOSITE PAGE
Stump fence, Maine, ca. 1890

BELOW
Worm fence, Stafford, Connecticut, 1810

Fenced farmstead, 1876

Wooden fences were used in both England and Holland and can be seen in seventeenth-century landscape depictions from both countries. However, they probably were not common because of timber shortages in these countries. Hedges or even ditches were used more often.

The vast New England forests must have been staggering for English settlers accustomed to conserving wood back home. The surfeit of timber "meant being warm in the winter, warmer even than the nobility of England could hope to be."[11] It also reshaped the colonists' building techniques.

Except for the very first rudimentary dwellings, houses in New England were almost invariably made entirely of wood. Instead of building outer walls made of wooden frameworks filled in with clay, typical of English half-timbered construction, outer walls in New England were sheathed in clapboards or shingles.

Stone, with which nature had also supplied New England in abundance, was rarely used to build houses, despite English traditions. Undoubtedly, speed of construction influenced this choice, but it was also at least partly due to the scarcity of lime, which was needed for mortar.[12] Stone walls built without mortar, however, became the most enduring fence type of the region. Building stone walls was slow and laborious, but they required less upkeep than wooden fences and lasted much longer; many survive to this day.

Although stone fences were used in the seventeenth century, the heaviest period of stone wall construction came much later, after the Revolution. A sad footnote to all the labor invested in building stone walls came in the 1830s with the invention of the McCormick reaper and other farm machinery best adapted to open expanses. Most New England fields enclosed by stone walls were too small for this equipment—often only two or three acres—and they were rendered obsolete for cultivation.

The abundance of trees in New England was a mixed blessing because it necessitated the hard work of clearing the land for cultivation. During the initial stages of land clearing, colonists made barriers by piling up brush around the field. This was usually temporary, but it showed the intent to enclose the field.[13] Sometimes the settlers made a peculiar-looking but impenetrable fence by lining up the stumps uprooted from the field along the perimeter, with the roots radiating outward. The interlacing roots kept out almost anything. Though these stump fences appear primitive, they are sometimes seen in nineteenth-century prints and photographs.

The post-and-rail fence was used in seventeenth-century England, and many colonial New England field fences were probably of this type. Two, three, or four parallel horizontal rails were inserted into holes in the posts, which were usually made of chestnut or red cedar to prevent rot. The space between the rails had to be narrow enough to keep out the notorious hogs. The post-and-rail fence did not need to have a gate, because rails could be pulled out and lowered to allow passage.

An innovative fence type that emerged was the worm, or zigzag, fence. There were other types of fences too, and the variety of fence styles persisted. One of the most striking features of nineteenth-century landscape engravings, drawings, and paintings is the multiplicity of fence styles on a single farm or along a single street. Once individual farms were established, fences proliferated, as they were needed to separate each function on the farm: cornfields, hay fields, pastures, barnyards, orchards, and gardens.

The role of the fence evolved as settlements increased and the wilderness was subdued. Fences were used less and less for defense and more and more to delineate property lines, especially as the common field system of the early towns was gradually abandoned. Division of land into smaller, individually owned parcels increased the number of fences as each farmer fenced in his own property, along with the different fields and yards within its borders. The once-common lands were thus divided and subdivided many times over, and fences and stone walls multiplied across the New England landscape.

1. Vanessa E. Patrick, "Partitioning the Landscape: The Fence in Eighteenth Century Virginia" (Williamsburg, Va.: Department of Architectural Research, Colonial Williamsburg Foundation, 1983), 9.

2. Alexander Young, ed., *Chronicles of the Pilgrim Fathers of the Colony of Plymouth, from 1602 to 1625* (Boston: Little and Brown, 1841), 284. Regarding dates before 1753, the first year denotes Old Style dating, when the year started in March, and the second year reflects modern usage.

3. Sydney V. James, Jr. ed., *Three Visitors to Early Plymouth: Letters about the Pilgrim Settlement in New England During Its First Seven Years* (Plymouth: Plimoth Plantation, 1983), 9.

4. William F. Robinson, *Coastal New England: Its Life and Past* (Boston: New York Graphic Society, 1983), 15.

5. Emmanuel Altham letter, in James, 24.

6. Samuel de Champlain, *Voyages of Samuel de Champlain*, vol. 3, trans. Charles Otis Pomeroy (1882; reprint, N.Y.: Burt Franklin, 1967), 138.

7. Personal communication with David Wagner, artist/historian, Thompson, Conn., 4 Dec. 1995.

8. *Winthrop Papers 1623-1630*, vol. 2 (Boston: Massachusetts Historical Society, 1931), 140-41.

9. Public Records of the Colony of Connecticut: Prior to the Union with New Haven Colony, May 1665. (Hartford: Brown Parsons, 1850), 518. Colonial usage of the word *cattle* often meant livestock in general.

10. Fairfield Historical Society, Fairfield, Conn., Town Records, 1661-1689, 18 Feb. 1677-78.

11. William Cronon, *Changes in the Land: Indians, Colonists, and the Ecology of New England* (N.Y.: Hill and Wang, 1983), 25.

12. Lecture by Marilyn Ackerman, "Colonial Connecticut: Construction and Rehabilitation," Woodbury, Connecticut, 4 Nov. 1995, sponsored by Connecticut Trust for Historic Preservation.

13. Susan Allport, *Sermons in Stone: Stone Walls of New England and New York* (N.Y.: W.W. Norton & Co., 1990), 35.

THE **WORM** **FENCE**

Gary Kulik

Fences are such commonplace objects, so largely lacking in interest for late-twentieth-century men and women, that it is difficult to recover just how significant they were, how much work they entailed, and how much capital they embodied for early settlers. More than any other object, fences marked the difference between European and Native American peoples, between private and common rights. In time, American fencing practice came to be different from past English practice. In an environment where cattle and swine grazed freely and in the absence of herders, many Americans designed their fences to keep livestock out rather than in. The law, in its initial expression, protected the interests of the owners of grazing animals. Property owners were obliged to build sound fences, subject to the judgment of town fence-viewers, to protect their interests. The twin effects of agricultural practice and the law helped to spur the construction of fences.[1]

Europeans were close students of American fences. Many offered detailed descriptions, complete with critiques and occasional praise, of American practice. What struck the earliest observers was the extraordinary amounts of wood Americans used to build their fences; according to one estimate, it took approximately two miles of fence to enclose a 160-acre square with a worm, or zigzag, fence. Europeans were certainly familiar with wooden fences. Eighteenth-century Swedes, for example, employed post-and-rail corrals to enclose their livestock, and there is some evidence of the Finns' use of worm fencing. German farmers in the early eighteenth century commonly employed board fences, but they also built

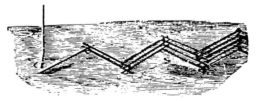

OPPOSITE PAGE
Worm fence, 1800

ABOVE
Building a worm fence

TOP
Rail fences, Orange,
Massachusetts, 1839

ABOVE
Farmstead,
Nicholas County,
West Virginia, 1927

rail fences with stone or wood posts, woven fences of oak and willow, stone walls, and planted hedges. In England, the latter two forms predominated. Limestone walls were common in Derbyshire, but elsewhere white hawthorn hedges with a shallow ditch on one or both sides and sometimes interspersed with ash and elm trees divided fields.[2]

Americans planted hedges relatively infrequently. Stone walls appear common only in New England and New York in the late eighteenth and early nineteenth centuries. The available evidence suggests that New Englanders too built first in wood, turning to stone only after years of extensive cutting in the settled portions of the region.[3]

Some settlers tried to build the fence forms they knew. Swedish naturalist Peter Kalm, visiting the Philadelphia area in the early 1750s, talked with several old Swedish settlers who had tried to build fences in the Swedish style. The fences failed because the posts quickly decayed. Kalm noted that farmers around Philadelphia employed a post-and-rail fence similar to the Swedish corral fence. But the posts rotted in the soil after only four to six years. Americans used large trees, not the small ones common to Sweden. Combined with the "unbelievable quantity of wood burned night and day," Kalm wrote, "one sees what punishment the forest is taking and wonders how it will look in thirty or fifty years."[4]

Until the last quarter of the nineteenth century, Americans built fences in a great variety of forms, but wood was the predominant material. Board fences were frequently used to enclose gardens, orchards, and animals. Post-and-rail fences, sometimes combined with ditches, were used to enclose tilled fields. Americans even experimented with the use of brush and tree stumps planted on the edges of their properties.[5] Near Albany, Kalm noted the use of deals, tree trunks squared with axes where they fell and laid between posts of white pine.

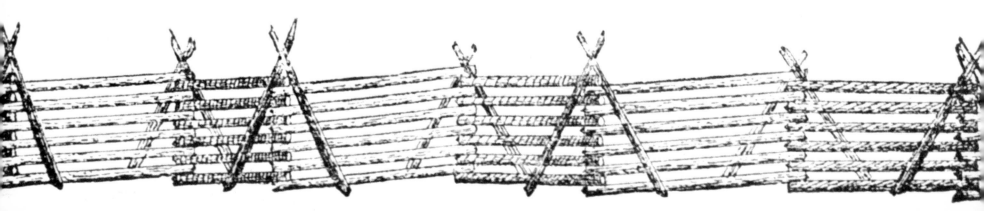

Between Saratoga and Albany, farmers used cross-notched logs as fences. Such systems, Kalm noted, were possible only because of the local abundance of wood.[6]

One form of wooden fence, however, consistently attracted the eyes of Europeans. Kalm called it the "worm fence of the Englishman," by which he meant English settlers. He noted that it was "commonly used in Pennsylvania, New Jersey, and New York." Unlike most fences, the worm fence had no posts. It took its name from its zigzag shape, which increased stability. Farmers laid a rail eleven feet long and four to six inches thick on the ground, sometimes placing its ends on stones to prevent rot. They then stacked eight to nine rails to form each section. The ends of the rails overlapped those in the adjoining sections. Other, and likely later, versions of the fence were secured with crossed diagonal stakes at each intersection.[7] The worm fence seems to have been widely used to enclose fields, especially pasture.

Folklore credits Virginians with the invention of the worm fence. William Tatham claimed in 1800 that it was "originally of Virginia." There seems no doubt that the form was more prevalent in the southern and in the mid-Atlantic colonies, spreading westward from there. Yet a closer look at the evidence suggests that the form appeared in the mid-Atlantic colonies prior to emerging in the South. The *Dictionary of American English* notes that the term appeared in the East Hampton, Long Island, records in 1652; the Salem, New Jersey, records note that a "new worme fence" enclosed the meeting house on Alloway's Creek in 1685, the same date as the earliest known Virginia reference. Numerous European travelers wrote about the worm fence, offering detailed descriptions and even drawings. Their comments, some as explicit as Kalm's, suggest that it was a distinctive American form. The *Oxford English Dictionary* recognizes the term as American.[8]

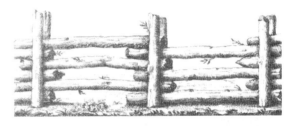

Castiglioni's illustrations of fences in Virginia and Pennsylvania, 1787

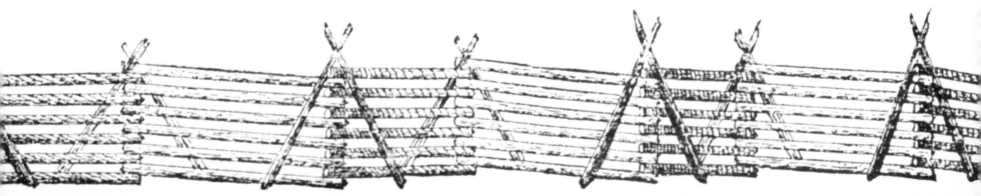

Worm fence, ca. 1900

Over the years, the worm fence has attracted a small amount of scholarly attention. Scholars have argued that it is an indigenous American form, and more recently, a Finnish form, but the evidence for either argument is weak. Scholars such as Wilbur Zelinsky, John Stilgoe, and the environmental historian Michael Williams argue its essential Americanness. Stilgoe, however, sees it as a regional style, an expression of Southern material culture. All three see it in some fashion as the innovative response of pioneers.[9]

Whatever its origins, there is no question of its impact. By 1870, it was the predominant fence type throughout the South, comprising over ninety percent of all fencing in North Carolina, South Carolina, Georgia, Alabama, Florida, Mississippi, Arkansas, and Tennessee, and over eighty percent in Ohio, Indiana, Kentucky, and West Virginia. It constituted over seventy percent of all fences in Virginia, and more than sixty percent in Pennsylvania. Only in New England and New York was it a minority form.[10]

The Italian traveler Castiglioni articulated the appeal of the worm fence. "They are preferred," he wrote, "because they require very little work." The Englishman William Oliver, writing forty years later, reinforced the point. "At first sight the worm fence appears very inefficient," he wrote, "but on closer inspection... it improves in one's estimation and would certainly be difficult for the pioneer settler to substitute anything so efficient and at the same time so easily got."[11] Scholars have largely accepted the argument. Michael Williams has developed it most thoroughly. The worm fence was resource-intensive and laborsaving. Americans who built it in such numbers were substituting relatively cheap wood for relatively dear labor. The cost in terms of forest cutting, as Kalm had noticed early, was high. It took 15,000 rails, ten rails per ten-foot section, to enclose a 160-acre square with a worm fence, and only 8,800 rails to do so with a post-and-rail fence.[12]

Worm fences did take considerably less time and effort to assemble. Post-and-rail fences required post holes and mortises. By one estimate, four slaves could build thirty-five to forty panels of post-and-rail fence in a day. Worm fences required no posts and could be laid up far more quickly. A male and female slave working together could build one hundred panels of worm fence in a day; a four-person crew could build two hundred. At standard day labor rates in the early nineteenth century, a farmer could fence a 160-acre square with worm fencing for $30, while the cost of a post-and-rail fence would be $48.[13]

Worm fences, however, used considerably more wood, and thus more rails had to be split. Estimates vary. Thomas Jefferson had a man who could split three hundred chestnut rails a day. But other estimates suggest that one hundred rails was a good day's work; two hundred was the pace of a strong farmer. At two hundred rails a day, it would take a farmer seventy-five days to split the rails necessary to enclose 160 acres with a worm fence and only forty-four days if he chose a post-and-rail fence. The extra time spent splitting rails entirely negated the savings in assembly. Assuming a two-man crew, it would take eighty-eight days to complete the post-and-rail fence and ninety days for the worm fence. The total cost of fencing a 160-acre square in worm fencing was therefore $90 ($60 of that for rails); the cost of rails and assembly for a post-and-rail fence of the same dimensions was approximately $83 ($35 of that for rails). If we add to the latter sum the cost of posts, the difference in total cost narrows further, disproving the contemporary observation that worm fencing was substantially cheaper than post-and-rail fencing.[14]

Yet the evidence suggests that Americans continued to believe that worm fencing was cheaper and laborsaving. Why? Perhaps farmers discounted the extra work of splitting rails. The work was different in character and could be spread out over long winter months. One Illinois farmer did just that, cutting fifty rails a day and laying them along the boundaries of his farm in preparation for spring assembly. Perhaps farmers saw the extra splitting as less onerous than the intensive, back-straining work of digging holes and setting posts. Ease of assembly clearly mattered. In addition, worm fences were easier to move and lasted longer than post-and-rail fences, thus lowering long-term costs.[15]

In the end, however, worm fencing cannot be explained as a simple matter of cost-effectiveness. The reasons for its popularity are more likely cultural. The earliest European observers were acute critics of the wasteful and prodigal

> Wherever a farm may be located,
> or whatever may be its production,
> fence, fence, fence, is the first,
> the intermediate, and the last
> consideration in the whole routine
> of the operations of the farm.
>
> Edward Todd,
> *Young Farmer's Manual*
> (1860)

Driving fence posts

Worm-fence... may fairly be ranked as the national fence, though it is temporary, giving way gradually to kinds requiring less lumber, and covering less land, as well as making a less awkward appearance not at all indicative of the straight-forwardness of the American character.

Report of the Commissioner of Agriculture for the Year 1871

habits of American farmers. Worm fences were not just extravagant in their use of wood; their configuration reduced the area that could be tilled and increased the growth of weeds. Their construction made them more likely to need repair. During the last half of the nineteenth century, the cost of worm fences grew too high to supply the needs of a country rapidly expanding across the Great Plains. By the 1850s, experiments were underway with wire fences, and ultimately wire would come to supersede wood fences of all kinds.[16]

Yet for upwards of two hundred years, the worm fence distinctively marked the fields of American farmers. Americans preferred the form, though for reasons that cannot be simply reduced to economics. The extraordinary availability of wood coupled with the desire to clear and fence equally extraordinary acreages, helped to create an environment conducive to both innovation and thoughtlessness, traits that remain with us.

TOP
Cutting points of
fence posts, ca. 1900

ABOVE
Illinois farmstead,
1874

1. William Cronon, *Changes in the Land: Indians, Colonists, and the Ecology of New England* (N.Y.: Hill and Wang, 1983), 134-35.

2. Michael Williams, *Americans and their Forests: A Historical Geography* (Cambridge: Cambridge University Press, 1989), 72; W.B. Hoskins, *The Making of the English Landscape* (London: Hodden and Stoughton, 1955), 195-200; Esther Louise Larson, "Pehr Kalm's Observations on the Fences of North America," *Agricultural History* 21 (1947): 75-78; Wilbur Zelinsky, "Walls and Fences," *Landscape* 8 (1959): 14-20; Terry G. Jordan and Matti Kaups, *Backwoods Frontier: An Ethnic and Ecological Interpretation* (Baltimore: Johns Hopkins University Press, 1989), 105-15; Henry Glassie, *Pattern in the Material Folk Culture of the Eastern United States* (Philadelphia: University of Philadelphia Press, 1968), 225-28; George A. Martin, *Fences, Gates, and Bridges* (N.Y.: O. Judd Co., 1887; reprint, Brattleboro, Vt.: Alan C. Hood & Co., Inc., 1992), 7-17; H.F. Raup, "The Fence in the Cultural Landscape," *Western Folklore* 1 (Jan. 1947): 1-7.

3. Cronon, 119-20.

4. Larson, 75-78.

5. J. Richie Garrison, *Landscape and Material Life in Franklin County, Massachusetts, 1770-1860* (Knoxville: University of Tennessee Press, 1991), 118-22; Bernard Herman, *The Stolen House* (Charlottesville: University Press of Virginia, 1992), 139-55.

6. Herman, 77.

7. Larson, 75-78.

8. William Tatham, *An Historical and Practical Essay on the Culture and Commerce of Tobacco* (London, 1800), reprinted in G. Melvin Herndon, *William Tatham and the Culture of Tobacco* (Coral Gables, Fla.: University of Miami Press, 1969), 10-11; *Oxford English Dictionary*; Rev. John Clayton to Robert Boyle, 1685, The Boyle Papers, Archives of the Royal Society of London, cited in Vanessa E. Patrick, "Partitioning the Landscape: The Fence in Eighteenth Century Virginia" (Williamsburg, Va.: Department of Research, Colonial Williamsburg Foundation, 1983), 36-37.

9. Zelinsky, 14-20; John Stilgoe, *Common Landscape of America* (New Haven: Yale University Press, 1982), 188-91; Williams, 69-72; Douglas Leechman, "Good Fences Make Good Neighbors," *Canadian Geographical Journal* 47 (1953): 218-35; Jordan and Kaups, 105-15.

10. U.S.D.A., *Report of the Commissioner of Agriculture for the Year 1871* (Washington, D.C., 1872), 497-512.

11. Luigi Castiglioni, *Viaggio: Travels in the United States of North America*, trans. and ed., Antonio Pace (Syracuse: Syracuse University Press, 1983), 319, n. 76; William Oliver, *Eight Months in Illinois* (Newcastle-upon-Tyne, 1843; reprint, Ann Arbor: University Microfilms, 1966), 131.

12. Williams, 72.

13. Williams, 72.

14. Williams, 72.

15. Oliver, 39-40; John Mason Peck, *A Guide for Emigrants* (Boston, 1831; reprint, N.Y.: Arno Press, 1975), 125; Allen G. Bogue, *From Prairie to Corn Belt: Farming on the Illinois and Iowa Prairies in the Nineteenth Century* (Chicago: University of Chicago Press, 1963), 74-75, 80, 244-45; Eugene Cotton Mather and John Fraser Hart, "Fences and Farms," *Geographical Review* 44 (1954): 201-23.

16. Clarence H. Danhof, "The Fencing Problem in the Eighteen-fifties," *Agricultural History* 18 (1944): 168-86.

THE **PICKET FENCE** AT **HOME**

Philip Dole

Though the fence ranks among the minor matters of building, it is far from being unimportant. Without it no residence can be properly protected, or regarded as complete. Its style and condition often indicate, unmistakenly, the taste and habits of the owner... the fence should enhance rather than impair the house." So wrote Henry Cleaveland in 1869, in *Village and Farm Cottages: Requirements of American Village Homes*, devoting five pages to the discussion of wood fences, including those of pickets.[1] At that time, in landscapes across the nation, from the East coast to the West, in towns and in the country, white-painted picket fences played a large part in the definition of private and public spaces.[2]

Successive waves of immigrants had made the picket fence a symbol of settlement. In America, individualism and privacy held special significance. In no other country had it been as possible for ordinary people to own land and build their own homes. From the late eighteenth century, facilitated by such laws as the Homestead Act of 1862, public land acquisitions opened more than four-fifths of North America to settlement. Required improvements immediately led to fence building, and with these structures came symbolic statements. The front fence became a signature of individual achievement and propriety. With a beautiful fence, "privacy and a proper regard for one's neighbors are expressed in faultless fashion."[3]

The picket fence has had a long history in many parts of the world. In the seventeenth century, the English and the Spanish transported their fence

OPPOSITE PAGE
Square picket fence, built ca. 1870, Roseburg, Oregon

ABOVE
Fence of pointed boards, built eighteenth century, Johnson, New York

ABOVE
Picket fence and
residence, Rochester,
Illinois, 1871

OPPOSITE PAGE
Picket fence, Lowell,
Massachusetts, 1911

traditions to the New World, primarily in the form of *palisades*—wooden constructions of pointed stakes, or logs, as much as twenty feet high, placed side by side—and occasionally as the more domestic picket. *Pale*, *paling*, *palisade*, and *picket* are related words, sharing origins and connotations, and they were used interchangeably into the nineteenth century. For each, the image is of a pointed stake or stick; a picket fence is made up of vertical pieces with projecting points, the top ends exposed, not covered.

Origins of North American picket fences can be traced to two broad, interrelated sources.[4] One source was the fortification or palisade. Americans used fences to contain and exclude in private yards as well as frontier garrisons. Pointed stakes, six feet high, surrounded the Louis Bolduc house in St.Genevieve, Missouri, for protection from Indians and "the flow of cattle along the streets."[5] Thomas Jefferson indicated the defensive role of the fence in describing one for a vegetable garden: "The ground laid off for my garden is to be enclosed with a Picquet fence ... seven feet high and so close that a hare can not get into it."[6] Defense on the domestic scale was from strays and marauders such as boys, cows, and chickens. It had long been noted that, for strength and protection, vertical boards were better than horizontal. The protective role of the good domestic fence led to its height and substantialness. From such utilitarian sources as the palisade came the domestic picket of pointed boards (three, four, or more inches wide) as well as that propensity, decorative in its result, to give fences an undulating or a chevron like upper edge through the use of pickets of varying lengths.

The second source for picket fences was literary and intellectual. Ideas presented in architectural publications stressed architectural roles and emphasized practical objectives. Earlier American design sources were English publications, followed in the late eighteenth century and into the twentieth century by numerous, widely distributed American architectural or builders' publications. Architects' designs for fences on the great European estates had provided instructive models. A preponderance of American wooden picket fences go back to eighteenth-century interpretations of European constructions which had combined masonry and open ironwork.[7] From masonry piers had come tall posts—square, boxed, and crowned perhaps by an urn or sphere. From the masonry base had come the large, curblike baseboards in eight- or ten-foot lengths. Between posts and on the curb, recalling the estate fence of iron, stood narrow, turned or square, wood pickets—the square pickets with faces of an inch and

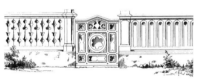

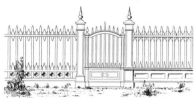

TOP
Fence with turned
posts and pickets,
Henry Failing
mansion, built 1876,
Portland, Oregon

ABOVE
Designs from *Model
Architect* by Samuel
Sloan, 1852

a quarter to two inches. These creations, four or five feet high, set the basis for many varieties of wooden picket fences in North America.

An example of the transfer of an English masonry-and-metal fence design to American constructions in wood is demonstrated by a number of superb architectural fences designed and built by Samuel McIntire in Salem, Massachusetts, about 1790. McIntire, like many designers, referred to his own library for assistance.[8] Batty Langley's *City and Country Builder's and Workman's Treasury of Designs*, published in London, undoubtedly inspired the McIntire fences for the Elias Derby house, the Pierce-Nichols house, and others.[9] Langley's text and McIntire's constructed fences are two examples that reinforced the understanding that magnificent fences were appropriate for places of importance.

Asher Benjamin, the widely publicized and emulated American author and builder, named his five elegant designs "front fences" in the *Practical House Carpenter* of 1830. Benjamin's wooden fences featured great posts and heavy bases supporting free interpretations of wooden grilles and latticework, "suitable for the enclosure of a country residence."[10] A twentieth-century critic summarized, "The fence is often an integral part of the approach, an introduction to the details and motifs to be found in the entrance and in the house itself."[11] Such concepts provide some explanation for the great height, substantial construction, and extensive length of many American picket fences, even ones designed for isolated farmhouses.

The front fence was the line between a public and a private place; a gate marked the transition from one to the other. "Unless you wish to invoke curses on your head... don't let your gates swing outward!" wrote Henry Cleaveland. Apparently most gates did; Samuel McIntire's gates, however, swung inward. To enhance reception, tall, boxed piers framed many gateways. A more pronounced entrance might be created by enlarging the gateway as an *aedicula*—an architectural form related to a niche or shrine —providing a useful, ceremonial symbol for the moment of entering. Some carpenters built wooden archways; others built pilastered or columnar frames roofed with a pediment, detailed with urns or a keystone. The commemorative west gate to Washington Park in Salem, Massachusetts, which Samuel McIntire built in 1802, was a large, segmental wooden archway carried on columnar piers, with a carved medallion of Washington below the pediment and a freestanding carved and gilded eagle above.[12] A classical double-niched entrance structure stood over the gates leading to Darius

Cartwright's classical revival home in Lorane, Oregon.[13]

In proper concern for the public view, builders placed the best, more finished side of the picket fence outward to the street. In simpler fences, the vertical supports were kept behind the pickets. Builders placed the round or square wood posts, or shafts of quarried granite (as at Canterbury, a Shaker village in New Hampshire) on the side facing the house. In the more architectural fence, boxed posts, fully visible, rose above the pickets. In some fences, two rails supported the vertical pickets—turned, square, or flat boards. In many fences, however, three rails were used to receive pickets of several lengths. In some, the pickets were organized in patterns of alternating chevrons, as in the Henry Failing fence; others had long, convex curves from post to post.

"It is the relationship of the size and height of the pickets to the space between the pickets, the relationship of picket and spacing to the width and height and thickness of the posts that produce the beautiful proportions of a fence," with each element treated to conform to "the designer's feeling for lightness and grace."[14] The most successful proportions relate the fence to the size and character of the house and to its situation; for example, a larger fence stands before a house on elevated ground.[15] Perhaps in keeping with the scale of the landscape, "fences... referred to as the Cape Cod type... are usually lower than in the rest of New England."[16]

Through the later nineteenth and into the early twentieth centuries, a noticeable evolution in fence construction was the increased use of turned posts and of pickets in complex jigsaw or turned work. In towns, iron fences replaced many wooden fences. A new development for utilitarian situations was a wooden picket fence bound with wire.[17] At the same time, several early fence designs remained popular, changing little over decades of construction. Along with fences in the grand style of McIntire or Benjamin (with square or turned pickets), there was a continuing emphasis on the common pointed flat-board picket. Early publications introduced several kinds of pointed tops: *The Carpenters' Company of the City and County of Philadelphia 1786 Rule Book* listed on two pages elements of various "palisade" board fences.[18] Mass-produced wood pickets became commercially available with the advent of sash, door, and blind factories, which along with planing mills, appeared in many, even remote, areas in the 1850s. As late as 1905, a mail-order catalog of the Chicago-based Foster-Munger Company, "America's Greatest Sash and Door Factory," offered, in three- and four-foot board lengths, a choice of seven pointed picket patterns and four patterns of square pickets with

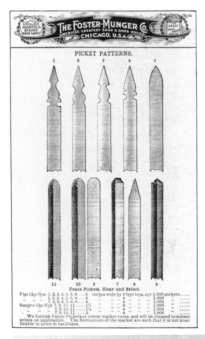

TOP
Mail-order pickets,
Chicago, 1905

ABOVE
Portable picket and wire
fence, Cleveland,
Oregon, 1916

31

Picket fences
between private
homes and public
spaces, Salem,
Massachusetts

Public buildings
with domestic-scale
fences, Freemasons
Hall and Church,
Mendocino,
California, ca. 1870

Closely spaced lower
boards contain hogs
and fowl, Gervais,
Oregon, 1860

shaped tops. In keeping with current fashion, the same catalog also offered several iron fences with pointed picket detail.[19]

There appeared to be an urge to domesticate every property, whether private or public, with fences. In towns, street edges with distinct, adjoining front-fence designs were characteristic, as seen in views of Mendocino, California, in 1868-1870. Larger houses, occupying full city blocks and surrounded by fences, had a presence almost matching that of the fenced-in courthouse or city church. A fence in keeping with the architectural style and scale of the house, and enclosing a full city block, was that for Henry Failing's house, built in Portland, Oregon, in 1876, designed by his San Francisco architect, Henry Cleaveland.[20] (Following completion of this house, Cleaveland turned his attention to the grounds, and Failing was sent sketches of eight or nine fence designs to consider, accompanied by the architect's terse comments on character and cost. Only Cleaveland's comments survive. Clearly Cleaveland sent a range and variety of designs to educate and direct the client: "No. 2 costs about $5—but I would not recommend it.") But it was the simple and ubiquitous domestic picket fence of pointed sticks painted white which made the full perimeter, stick after stick, of many city blocks, each enclosing a house, courthouse, or church. By 1876, ten county courthouses in Missouri were fenced with some sort of picket.[21]

For home grounds, fences emphasized the centrality of the house within its large, enclosed rectangle of yard, garden, and outbuildings—a world within a world. Across the front, facing a driveway or street, was the white picket fence with its formal gated entrance. When pickets were not carried around the perimeter, board fences enclosed the sides and back. This painted companion of the picket fence was usually composed of horizontal planks of incremental size and spacing. Carefully proportioned, with the widest planks at the bottom, the upper planks decreased in size as the spaces between them increased; the smallest plank and widest space was at the top. This was a common version of the post-and-rail fence— rail referring to horizontal members, here boards. Board fencing in the barnyard is used with a picket fence at the Sam Brown house built in 1860 at Gervais, Oregon. Effective in containing wandering fowl, the horizontal board fence was effective visually, too. It was sometimes used as a front fence and was frequently used in American towns as well as on farms.

On many farms, a trinity of fences—rail, horizontal board, picket, one within the other—described three different but concentric zones. Split rails surrounded the distant pastures; board fences bounded barnyards or backyards; at the house stood the picket fence.[22] This combination, an established custom on the Eastern Seaboard, seen at Connecticut farms in the 1830s, migrated west; examples are found in Iowa, Kansas, Oregon, Washington, and elsewhere.[23] There are variations, as in areas where stone walls, not rails, make the outer fence. But the picket fence marked the operational center of most farm acreages—the farmhouse itself, home.

Not all theorists recommended that homes have front fences. Severe opposition came from the influential and revered landscape architect Andrew Jackson Downing, whose *Treatise on the Theory and Practice of Landscape Gardening*, published in 1841, was republished in ten editions through 1879. He devotes only one of 570 pages to fences. Downing wrote, "Nothing is more common, than a display immediately around the dwelling of spruce paling... an abomination among the fresh fields, of which no person of taste could be found guilty... a perversity. The close proximity of fences to the house gives the whole place a confined and mean character."[24] Others, such as the next generation's arbiter, Frank J. Scott, writing in 1870, expressed similar views. But as seen in both nineteenth-century photographs and contemporary illustrated American county histories, picket fences continued to predominate as the front fence and dooryard enclosure. By the early years of the twentieth century, except for a brief revival of picket fences accompanying Colonial Revival houses, popular responses to landscape theory sought to minimize boundaries and residential fences in order to share spaces and views and emulate natural settings. The picket fence all but disappeared. Many front yards opened up completely, for the major distinction between one home place and the next and between the home and the street had been removed.

A paradoxical use of domestic fences at forts in Washington State illustrate

Trinity of rail, board, and picket, Clayton County, Iowa, 1875

Commandant's house at
Fort Simcoe, Washington

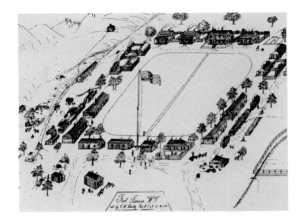

Fort Simcoe,
Washington, 1858

and symbolize the long-held and culturally imbedded feeling for home and fence. Conflicts between settlers and Indians around 1856 led the U.S. Army to build isolated outposts in the wilderness, far from "the States, back home." Beautifully detailed and constructed, these residences were an astonishing achievement— surprising in the builders' awareness and use of current architectural style, far from any major cultural center. They were also remarkable for the delivery of building materials to the sites; windows and other finish materials were transported over a specially constructed sixty-mile trail to Fort Simcoe. At Fort Steilacoom, fashionable cottages for officers were built in the "Ionic Style," each accompanied by its own picket fence.[25] There were no blockhouses. About three thousand feet of picket fence, domestic in scale, surrounded the fort, barracks, and officers' living quarters.

Four blockhouses did mark the outer corners of Fort Simcoe, yet without palisades or even fences between them. Officers' quarters of 1856-1858 were in a Gothic style.[26] The commandant's stylish home, "this pretty and conveniently arranged house," duplicated in wood Downing's "Villa Farmhouse."[27] Disregarding the picturesque possibilities of its setting and Downing's feeling about fences, a picket fence surrounded the commandant's home. The particularly American image of home, freestanding within a fenced yard, was complete and clear: Downing's theory notwithstanding, a home must have a fence.

1. Henry W. Cleaveland and William and Samuel Backus, *Village and Farm Cottages, the Requirements of American Village Homes* (N.Y.: Appleton, 1869), 157.

2. Philip Dole, *The Picket Fence In Oregon: An American Vernacular Comes West* (Eugene, Ore.: University Press,1986), 5.

3. Alfred Hopkins, "Fences & Fence Posts of Colonial Times," *The White Pine Series of Architectural Monographs* 8 (N.Y.: Marchbanks Press, 1922), 7.

4. Dole, 6.

5. Dole, 14.

6. Edwin Betts, ed., *Thomas Jefferson's Garden Book* (Philadelphia: American Philosophical Society, 1944), 467.

7. Dole, 7.

8. Fiske Kimball, *Mr. Samuel McIntire, Carver, the Architect of Salem* (Gloucester, Mass.: Peter Smith, 1966), 15.

9. Batty Langley, *The City and County Builder's and Workman's Treasury of Designs* (London,1750; reprint N.Y.: Benjamin Bloom, Inc.,1967), 15, plate 19.

10. Asher Benjamin, *The Practical House Carpenter* (1830; facsimile, N.Y.: DeCapo, 1972), 69.

11. Hopkins, 11.

12. John Warner Barber, *Historical Collections, of Every Town in Massachusetts* (Worcester: Warren Lazell, 1844), 225.

13. Albert G. Walling, *Illustrated History of Lane County* (Portland: A.G.Walling, 1884).

14. Carl F. Schmidt, *Fences, Gates and Garden Houses* (Rochester, N.Y.: By the Author, 1963), 13-15.

15. Benjamin, 69.

16. Hopkins, 11.

17. George A. Martin, *Fences, Gates, and Bridges* (N.Y.: O. Judd Co., 1909; reprint, Brattleboro, Vt.: Alan C. Hood & Co., Inc., 1992), 43.

18. *The Carpenters' Company of the City and County of Philadelphia 1786 Rule Book*, introduction by Charles E. Peterson (reprint, Philadelphia: Bell Pub. Co., 1971).

19. The Foster-Munger Company, *Official Catalog* (Chicago, 1905), 697.

20. Arthur W. Hawn, "The Henry Failing House," *Oregon Historical Quarterly* 82 (Winter 1981), 366.

21. Marian M. Ohman, *Encyclopedia of Missouri Courthouses* (Columbia, Mo.: University of Missouri, Columbia, 1981), unpaged.

22. Dole, 35.

23. John Warner Barber, *Historical Collections, of Every Town in Connecticut* (New Haven: Drurie and Peck, 1838), 395; A. T. Andreas, *Illustrated Historical Atlas of the State of Iowa* (1875; reprint Iowa Historical Society, n.d.); A. T. Andreas, *Illustrated Historical Atlas of the State of Minnesota* (1874; reprint Evansville, Ind.: Unigraphic, Inc.,1975); Edward C. Carter II, John C. Van Horne, Charles E. Brownell, eds., *Latrobe's View of America, 1795-1820* (New Haven: Yale University Press, 1985); W. E. Morrison, *History of Ontario County, New York* (1876; reprint Ovid, N.Y.: W. E. Morrison & Co.,1976).

24. Andrew Jackson Downing, *Treatise on the Theory and Practice of Landscape Gardening* (1859; reprint, N.Y.: Funk and Wagnalls, 1967), 295-296.

25. Tonkin/Greissinger/Architects, "Fort Steilacoom, Historic Structures Report, 1979-1980" (Washington State Office of Archaeology and Historic Preservation), 8.

26. Priscilla Knuth, *'Picturesque' Frontier: the Army's Fort Dalles* (Portland: Oregon Historical Society, 1966), 33.

27. H. Dean Guie, *Bugles in the Valley: Garnett's Fort Simcoe* (Portland: Oregon Historical Society, 1977), 107, 168-171.

AMERICA FENCED

Estella M. Chung and Gregory K. Dreicer

Fences... constitute a stabilizing force upon the landscape.

Eugene Cotton Mather and John Fraser Hart, "Fences and Farms" (1954)

The first man who, having fenced in a piece of land, said "This is mine,"and found people naive enough to believe him, that man was the true founder of civil society.

Jean Jacques Rousseau, *A Discourse on the Origin of Inequality* (1754)

Not the constitution, but free land and an abundance of natural resources open to a fit people, made the democratic type of society in America.

Frederick Jackson Turner,
The Frontier in American History (1920)

There are certain fundamental necessities which should go with every city [play]ground.

They are:

First, fence;

Second, shelter;

Third, toilet;

Fourth, water.

Recreation Bureau of the City of New York,
Annual Report (1910)

Home is for many, a model of our own universe, where we act out all the dramas of life—and often, of death—and where our possessions, some utilitarian, some for decoration, are signs of the things that matter to us.

Paul Olivier, "Houses are for Living In" (1990)

Place is security, space is freedom: we are attached to the one and long for the other.

Yi-Fu Tuan, *Space and Place: The Perspectives of Experience* (1977)

If a man owns land, the land owns him.

Ralph Waldo Emerson, *Wealth* (1860)

LIVE FENCES: HEDGES

Diana Balmori

Hedges are live fences. The term *hedge* means trees or shrubs growing closely together in a line, with their branches interlacing so that individual plants are not distinct and there is no room for passage through them. Though *hedge* can refer to fences around yards as well as agricultural fields, hedges properly belong to the domestic landscape. *Hedgerow* is the precise word for hedges in the agricultural landscape. Hedgerows were designed mainly to keep livestock in or out of a field, and to protect crops. Domestic hedges, however, identify property boundaries, protect property, and provide privacy. This essay traces the use of hedges in America, the reasons for their use, their subsequent decline, the recent revived interest in them, and our ecological reinterpretation of their functions.

Although there is some evidence for the existence of hedges in seventeenth-century America, there is firmer documentation of them in the eighteenth century. The Virginia Fence Act of 1705 accepted "a hedge two foot high, upon a ditch of three foot deep and three foot broad" as a legal fence. Hedges stood on the ground of the Governor's Palace in Williamsburg, Virginia, in 1779. In 1794, Thomas Jefferson replaced decayed fence rails at Monticello, his farm in Charlottesville, Virginia, with rows of peach trees to divide certain fields; other Monticello fields were defined by thorn hedges.[1]

But it was in the nineteenth century, especially in the Midwest, that the hedge played an important role. Hedges, or more precisely hedgerows, appeared in agricultural fields as a result of two forces: the scarcity of wood and the creation

OPPOSITE PAGE
Chatsworth Garden,
England

ABOVE
Hedgerow in field

Osage orange tree
and fruit

of laws governing fences and herding. Foraging livestock forced settlers to fence gardens and fields before the first harvest. The scarcity of timber in many places, particularly in the western margins of the prairie, led farmers to search for alternatives to traditional wood fences. Although the hedge had attracted attention in the East, it was not until the 1840s that it received public attention as the solution to the fencing problem. By the 1850s, it was used on a large scale in Ohio, Illinois, and Indiana.[2] The planting of hedges, particularly those of Osage orange, became so popular in the 1850s that the *Valley Farmer* coined the term "hedge mania."[3]

Territorial legislation recognized the hedge as a legal fence in 1857: "Any structure or hedge or ditch, in the nature of a fence, used for purposes of enclosure which is such as good husbandmen generally keep, and shall be testimony of skillful men, appear to be sufficient, shall be deemed a lawful fence."[4]

Although a wide variety of plants such as the wild rose and native American thorns were used, it was the Osage-orange hedge that dominated the western prairie.[5] The Osage-orange (*citronium maclura*) hedge could be established in three years and had long hard spines which deterred stock from attempting to get through. Of southern origin, it is a small tree which grows to about forty feet in height. It became the favored plant for hedges because of its hardiness in northern climates and for being relatively disease-free. The use of these plants spread quickly through the Midwest in the 1850s and 1860s. The decade following the Civil War saw a major extension of Osage-orange hedges in Nebraska and Kansas. By 1871, this kind of hedge ranked with post-and-rail and board fences among the three leading types of enclosure in Nebraska.[6] Advertisements for one million of the trees for sale at Baxter Springs, two million at Ottawa, and five million at Bonyshan County—all in Kansas—give a sense of the popularity of the plant, probably encouraged by tax reductions given to farmers who planted hedges.[7]

James Mossman, an enterprising farmer, offered his patented hedge-planting method in *The Live Fence and Timber Grower's Guide* of 1905. He proposed that his hedgerow serve not only as a fence but also as a source of wood.[8] People did not commonly patent hedgerows, but his proposal was based on having the hedgerow yield other benefits than the protection of an agricultural crop. He claimed that:

"By simply adopting the Mossman invention of utilizing the ground occupied by our fence... a strip six feet wide... [and] planting a row with one-year-old timber plant of Osage orange from one to two feet apart... cultivating and trimming for three years would include all the capital and labor required. In four years you will have grown an everlasting live fence that will stop horses, cattle, and sheep. We call it everlasting for when it becomes large enough to cut off for fence posts or timber, it will sprout up and reproduce itself much faster than the first growth did ... and in ten years you will have grown a crop of live fenceposts and live timber."[9]

Mossman added two strands of wire to the row of plants as a way of establishing the fence before the Osage oranges were fully grown in. The more elaborate method of establishing a hedge, which produced greater impenetrability, was that of *plashing* or *pleaching*. This method consists of cutting the main stalks of one- or two-year-old plants in the hedgerow halfway through, bending them at an angle, and tying them to a vertical post, thereby providing a criss-crossing of stalks that leaves no passage through the hedge. It was not as extensively used in America as it was in England, where hedgerow pleachers and trimmers became important agricultural craftsmen, and their tools, called *billhooks*, the mark of a region.

The use of Osage-orange hedges started to decline once the barbed-wire fence was developed and spread over the whole country in the 1880s. The hedge required careful planting and trimming, frequent cultivation, and protection from livestock during its first years. (In fact, many farmers actually built fences around their young hedges.) Hedges also fell victim to prairie fires.[10] Barbed wire required less upkeep and proved a more effective barrier against cattle. Although the Osage orange was no longer considered the solution to the fencing problem, it continued to be planted until the 1920s, probably because of its lower cost to the farmer.

In addition to maintenance requirements, hedges occupied large amounts of land and impeded the movement of farmers' large, motorized agricultural equipment. Farmers worldwide began to systematically remove thousands of miles of hedges from their fields. In England, a country where hedges were paramount, the losses have been so great that a law was passed to protect them. Until the 1970s, the government subsidized farmers to rip out hedges in the name of agricultural improvement. In response to this loss, the government launched a hedgerow incentive scheme in 1992. Farmers became eligible for grants of £1.50 to £2 a meter for planting hedges and practicing the traditional, and expensive, method of hedge pleaching. This new attitude toward hedges comes from recent studies of the ecological role of hedges in the landscape.

In the United States, there has been recent interest in monitoring the removal of hedgerows. Though the most active period of hedgerow removal was between the colonial settlement and 1940, rates of removal appear to have intensified since

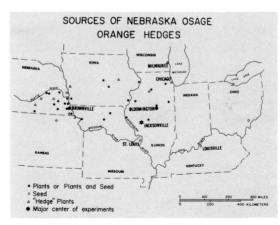

TOP
Sources of Nebraska
Osage orange plants

ABOVE
Hedged home,
built ca. 1860

the 1970s. Urban expansion and the construction of new roads, as well as the widening of old ones, are significant factors.

Though not yet well studied in the United States, the role of hedgerows in the agricultural landscape has been a focus of European researchers: "They have shown the reduction of windspeed leeward of hedgerows to a distance fifteen to twenty times the height of the windbreak, resulting in reduced rates of snowmelt and soil drying; generally, greater water use efficiency by plants' increased humidity, lower rates of evaporation and transpiration; wind erosion decreases, crop increases; and plants exhibit greater growth. They also have been seen to provide habitat for wildlife. Hedgerow timber is seen as important in localities deprived of woods. Aesthetic properties—least studied—have emerged in a search in the Netherlands where correlations have been shown between positive public attitudes toward the landscape and the presence and density of hedgerows."[11]

Richard T. Forman and Jacques Baudry's research on hedgerows summarizes their main ecological roles.[12] In the two graphs on this page, the first illustrates the results of the deflection of wind caused by the hedgerow, the resulting greater heat, and the diminished wind-speed in the field. The other graph shows the different bands and conditions of protected areas which the hedgerow provides at the varying distances (1 h = 1 hedgerow height).

In particular, the drawings illustrate the effect on the hedgerow border. By acting as conduits, they foster wildlife, permitting a variety of bugs, rodents, and small mammals to subsist in acres stripped of all other cover. The hedgerow functions as a lifeline for these species. The animals, in turn, enrich the plant variety of the hedgerow itself, which becomes the depository of a very diverse plant life that is protected from wind, machinery, and desiccation. Hedgerows also serve as connectors across the landscape, permitting species to escape enemies, reach another landscape, or escape from a declining one. At the same time, they may also serve as conduits for predators. Particularly in treeless environments, the removal of hedges brings about a decline in landscape diversity, fauna habitat, and shelter, and has an impact on crop yield, plant growth, and wind erosion. So just as the hedgerow seemed to have reached its end in the agricultural world, its aesthetic and environmental qualities have brought it back to life.

The creation of a new kind of park in America—the linear park—brings about an opportunity to reinstate the hedgerow while giving it an overt ecological role. Linear parks—also called greenways—are being created all across America on

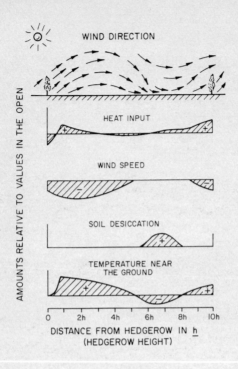

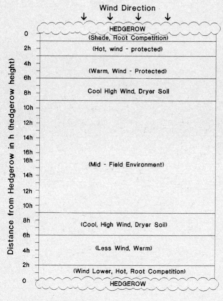

TOP AND ABOVE
Effects of hedgerows
on field

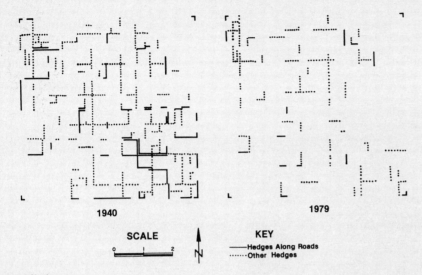

1940　　　　　　　　**1979**

SCALE　　　　　KEY
0   1   2　　——Hedges Along Roads
　　　　　　　······Other Hedges

Loss of hedgerows in
Nemaha County,
Nebraska

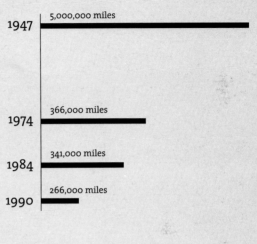

1947　5,000,000 miles

1974　366,000 miles

1984　341,000 miles

1990　266,000 miles

Loss of hedgerows
in England

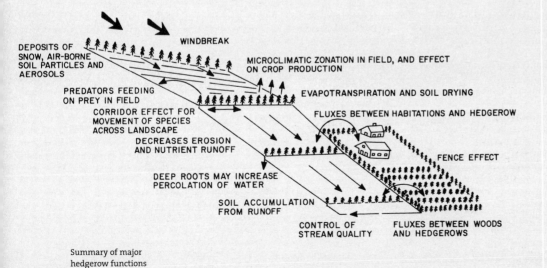

DEPOSITS OF
SNOW, AIR-BORNE
SOIL PARTICLES AND
AEROSOLS

WINDBREAK

MICROCLIMATIC ZONATION IN FIELD, AND EFFECT
ON CROP PRODUCTION

PREDATORS FEEDING
ON PREY IN FIELD

EVAPOTRANSPIRATION AND SOIL DRYING

CORRIDOR EFFECT FOR
MOVEMENT OF SPECIES
ACROSS LANDSCAPE

FLUXES BETWEEN HABITATIONS AND HEDGEROW

DECREASES EROSION
AND NUTRIENT RUNOFF

DEEP ROOTS MAY INCREASE
PERCOLATION OF WATER

FENCE EFFECT

SOIL ACCUMULATION
FROM RUNOFF

CONTROL OF
STREAM QUALITY

FLUXES BETWEEN WOODS
AND HEDGEROWS

Summary of major
hedgerow functions

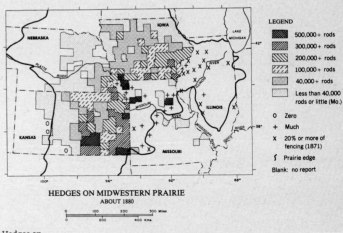

LEGEND

■ 500,000+ rods
▨ 300,000+ rods
▧ 200,000+ rods
▨ 100,000+ rods
▒ 40,000+ rods
□ Less than 40,000
　 rods or little (Mo.)

O　Zero
+　Much
X　20% or more of
　 fencing (1871)
ʃ　Prairie edge

Blank: no report

HEDGES ON MIDWESTERN PRAIRIE
ABOUT 1880

0   100   200   300 Miles
0   200   400 Kms.

Hedges on
Midwestern prairie,
ca. 1880

narrow corridors of land recovered for civic use from abandoned railroads, utility corridors, and river banks. The continuity of hedgerows along this new, linear, civic space—which connects the city, suburb, and open country—provides a haven for wildlife and plants. As highways and traffic cut the landscape into impassable channels for wildlife, the invention of the linear park may provide safe passageways over longer and longer landscape ribbons. While not offering complete continuity—gaps will exist for each new entry point—hedges can take on the role of a protective cover for many species along large sections of urban, suburban, and agricultural landscapes.

1. Vanessa E. Patrick, "Partitioning the Landscape: The Fence in Eighteenth Century Virginia" (Williamsburg, Va.: Department of Architectural Research, Colonial Williamsburg Foundation, 1983), 39-40.

2. Clarence Danhof, "The Fencing Problem in the Eighteen-Fifties," *Agricultural History* 18 (1944), 181-82.

3. *Valley Farmer* 8 (Saint Louis, Mo., 1856).

4. Laws of Nebraska Territory, Third Session, 1857, enacted April 13, 1857, cited in Leslie Hewes, "Early Fencing on the Western Margin of the Prairie," *Nebraska History* 69 (1982): 342, n. 12.

5. Danhof, 180-81.

6. Hewes, 313.

7. Hewes, 328.

8. James Mossman, *The Live Fence and Timber Grower's Guide* (Westerville, Ohio: By the Author, 1905).

9. Mossman, 5.

10. Danhof, 183.

11. Bradley H. Baltensperger, "Hedgerow Distribution and Removal in Nonforested Regions of the Midwest" *Journal of Soil and Water Conservation* 42 (1987): 60-64.

12. Richard T.T. Forman and Jacques Baudry, "Hedgerows and Hedgerow Networks in Landscape Ecology," *Environmental Management* 8 (1984): 495-510.

OPPOSITE PAGE
Hedge clipping, Greenbelt, Maryland, 1946

BELOW
Farmington Canal model

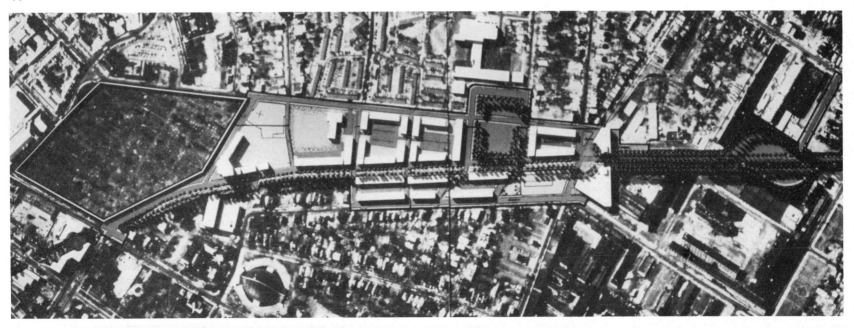

FENCING

ROBERT FROST'S

Anne M. Lange

Robert Frost may be the only American poet to have composed a modern proverb: "Good fences make good neighbors." Although the idea can be traced to *Poor Richard's Almanac*, William Harmon notes that Frost recast it in his own language, and in this form, it has burned itself into our national consciousness.[1] More than eighty years after being written, Robert Frost's poem "Mending Wall" provokes wrangling between two U.S. Supreme Court Justices over its meaning, the fence-building industry adopts "Good fences make good neighbors" as its motto, and a sign appears in a Sarajevan suburb, "Good Fence Makes Good Friends." As they say in Hollywood, this poem "has legs."

Literary critics have also been divided in their interpretations of this forty-five-line poem, some siding with the poem's narrator, who questions the need for walls, and others defending the fence-loving neighbor, whom they view as unfairly maligned. Edmund Jayne, in a far-out interpretation, says the poem represents "a sublimated homosexual relationship between two men separated by the wall."[2]

After reading it once or numerous times, one is left with the question: which position is correct? The problem lies with the ambivalence of the narrator, arising from Frost's own ambivalence toward the need for walls. Although the

Something there is that doesn't love a wall,
That sends the frozen-ground-swell under it
And spills the upper boulders in the sun,
And makes gaps even two can pass abreast.
The work of hunters is another thing:
I have come after them and made repair
Where they have left not one stone on a stone,
But they would have the rabbit out of hiding,
To please the yelping dogs. The gaps I mean,
No one has seen them made or heard them made,
But at spring mending-time we find them there.
I let my neighbor know beyond the hill;
And on a day we meet to walk the line
And set the wall between us once again.
We keep the wall between us as we go.
To each the boulders that have fallen to each.
And some are loaves and some so nearly balls
We have to use a spell to make them balance:
"Stay where you are until our backs are turned!"
We wear our fingers rough with handling them.
Oh, just another kind of outdoor game,
One on a side. It comes to little more:
There where it is we do not need the wall:
He is all pine and I am apple orchard.

WITH MEANING

"MENDING WALL"

My apple trees will never get across
And eat the cones under his pines, I tell him.
He only says, "Good fences make good neighbors."
Spring is the mischief in me, and I wonder
If I could put a notion in his head:
"*Why* do they make good neighbors? Isn't it
Where there are cows? But here there are no cows.
Before I built a wall I'd ask to know
What I was walling in or walling out,
And to whom I was like to give offense.
Something there is that doesn't love a wall,
That wants it down." I could say "Elves" to him,
But it's not elves exactly, and I'd rather
He said it for himself. I see him there,
Bringing a stone grasped firmly by the top
In each hand, like an old-stone savage armed.
He moves in darkness as it seems to me,
Not of woods only and the shade of trees.
He will not go behind his father's saying,
And he likes having thought of it so well
He says again, "Good fences make good neighbors."

From *The Poetry of Robert Frost: Collected Poems, Complete and Unabridged*,
edited by Edward Connery Lathem. N.Y.: Holt, Rinehart and Winston, 1969.

narrator questions the need for walls, he is the one who initiates the spring wall-mending ritual. In addition, he has mended the wall by himself during the preceding hunting season. He doesn't tell his neighbor how he really feels; most of the poem is a rumination. In the final section of the poem, however, the narrator's apparent congeniality toward his neighbor changes abruptly. It starts with him observing the simple act of his neighbor lifting a rock: "I see him there, / Bringing a stone grasped firmly by the top / In each hand," which is followed by a menacing simile: "like an old-stone savage armed." Then comes another sinister characterization: "He moves in darkness, as it seems to me, / Not of woods only and the shade of trees." The cooperative act of jointly mending the wall has been soured by the speaker's dark imagination. The poem ends on a condescending note: "And he likes having thought of it so well / He says again, "Good fences make good neighbors." A.R. Coulthard observes that "the narrator and the author of "Mending Wall" don't come across nearly so well as Frost probably thought."[3]

Many critics assume that Frost and the narrator share the same viewpoint. However, the circumstances of the writing of this poem discourage drawing parallels to the writer's life experience. In 1912, at age thirty-eight, after having failed as a farmer but succeeded as a teacher, Frost decided to go abroad in the

hope of becoming a full-time poet. He and his wife Elinor headed for England with their four children to "live under thatch" and stayed until 1915. Frost wrote "Mending Wall" in 1913. He later recalled, "I wrote the poem 'Mending Wall' thinking of the old wall I hadn't mended in several years and which must be in a terrible condition... I was very homesick for my old wall in New England."[4] This homesick impulse, however, engendered no sentimental paean to a stone wall; instead Frost channeled this impulse and fashioned the complex narrative that is "Mending Wall." In addition, the neighbor in the poem is based on Napoleon Guay, Frost's French-Canadian neighbor in Derry, New Hampshire, with whom he got along very well. In fact it was Guay who looked after Frost's farm when he took several month-long vacations.[5]

Over the years, Frost's own statements on "Mending Wall" have revealed his ambivalence about the need for walls:

• 1947. Frost stated that his second favorite poem "would have to be 'Mending Wall'; good fences *do* make good neighbors, you know."[6]

• 1961. Before a trip to Israel, he said that the "boundary right in the middle" of Jerusalem troubled him. As to whether good fences make good neighbors: "It's the other fellow in the poem who says that... I don't know. Maybe I was both fellows in the poem."[7]

• 1962. In Moscow, after the erection of the Berlin Wall, Frost read "Mending Wall," and told his audience, "I've had lots of adventures with that poem. People are frequently misunderstanding it or misinterpreting it. The secret of what it means I keep."[8]

In his eighty-fifth year, Frost denied that "Mending Wall" was an allegory; he said it illustrated "the impossibility of drawing sharp lines and making exact distinctions between good and bad or between almost any two abstractions. There is no rigid separation between right and wrong."[9]

So Frost, by his own accounts, is either the fence-builder, the wall-toppler, neither, or "both fellows" in the poem. He believed that "all a man's art is a bursting unity of opposites."[10] Frost would probably prefer readers to decide for themselves which side of the fence to be on, or whether to tear it down.

1. William Harmon, ed., *The Classic Hundred: All-Time Favorite Poems* (N.Y.: Columbia University Press, 1990), 114.

2. A.R. Coulthard, "Frost's Mending Wall," *Explicator 45*, no. 2 (Winter 1987), 40.

3. Coulthard, 42.

4. Lawrance Thompson, *Robert Frost: The Early Years, 1874-1915* (N.Y.: Holt, Rinehart and Winston, 1966), 432-33.

5. Thompson, *Early Years*, 284-85.

6. N. Arthur Bleau, "Robert Frost's Favorite Poem," *Frost: Centennial Essays*, 3rd ed., Robert K. Miller, ed., *The Informed Argument: A Multidisciplinary Reader and Guide* (N.Y.: Harcourt Brace Jovanovich, 1986), 454.

7. Stanley Burnshaw, *Robert Frost Himself* (N.Y.: Braziller, 1986), 289.

8. Lawrance Thompson, *Robert Frost: The Later Years, 1938-1963*, (N.Y.: Holt, Rinehart and Winston, 1966), 316.

9. Burnshaw, 289.

10. Burnshaw, 289.

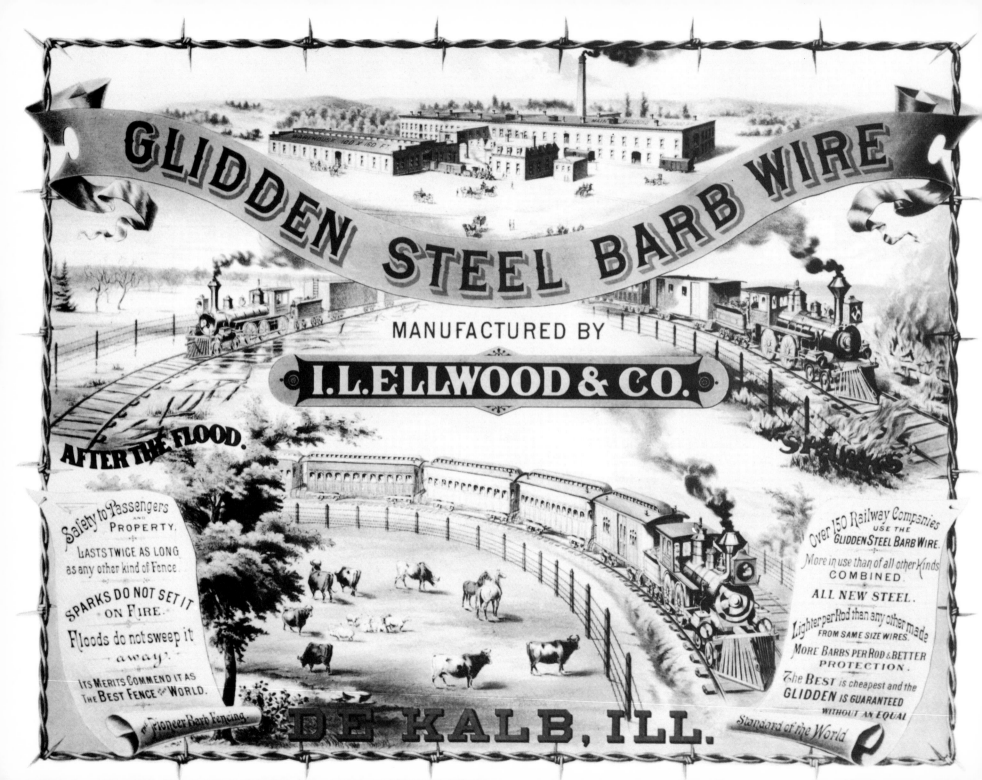

BARBED WIRE AND THE AMERICAN WEST

John B. Jackson

Throughout the nineteenth century, as new settlements came into being, the tyranny of fences was everywhere a matter of complaint. Fences cost money to build and maintain, and the scarcity of wood in the open regions of the Midwest was a serious handicap. Most disturbing of all was the effect of these costs on new settlers with little money. "When a score of young farmers go West," the Commissioner of Agriculture wrote in 1871, "with strong hands and little cash in them, but a munificent promise to each of a homestead worth $200... for less than $20 in land office fees, they often find that $1,000 will be spent to fence scantily each farm with little benefit to themselves, but mainly for mutual protection against a single stock grower, rich in cattle and becoming richer by feeding them without cost upon the unpurchased prairie."

The commissioner was referring to the recent invasion of Illinois, Iowa, and Kansas by itinerant cattle traders, who moved in on the treeless prairie region. At first, many of these traders accumulated their herds locally and gradually, but after the Civil War they were outnumbered by itinerant cattlemen from Texas who threatened to transform the prairie into a vast ranch enterprise from which they could drive their herds to eastern markets. Their impact was felt by local farmers, who could not compete with the southern traders and suffered from the invasion of their unfenced land by great numbers of foreign livestock.

The damage was not confined to the vacant prairies and unfenced portions of established farms; the roads were often crowded and made all but impassable

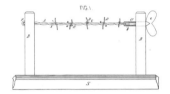

FIG I.

OPPOSITE PAGE
Barbed-wire
advertising poster,
ca. 1900

ABOVE
Joseph Glidden's
barbed-wire patent,
1874

Advertisement
featuring Joseph
Glidden

by wandering livestock. It was generally admitted in nineteenth-century America that our roads were the worst in any civilized nation: poorly planned, poorly constructed, and rarely, if ever, maintained in a safe condition. Much of this could be blamed on the practice of appointing road masters (as they were then called) from among local political worthies who were in office for no more than a year. The average road in the country was used as a place to deposit ashes and garbage and broken items of every sort. Farm vehicles were parked in the roadway, and household work took place in the road near the farm house. Even the roadside fences built by conscientious landowners contributed to the confusion: they served to catch and retain snow and to create drifts deep enough to discourage all travelers on foot. The wandering cattle did little to improve conditions, and a common complaint was that children on their way to school were terrified by cows and pigs that devoured front lawns and gardens, and defiled graveyards and public gathering places.

While fences were needed to exclude local strays and discourage Texas-style "drives," they were costly to build and maintain. Many communities drew up "herd laws" outlawing the unauthorized use of public lands or unfenced private lands by cattlemen, who were usually without land of their own. These laws were as much the work of village landowners as of irate farmers. They required cattlemen to hire herders (or cowboys) to control the cattle so that farmers would no longer need fences to protect their crops. The cattle dealers and the owners of stray cattle bitterly opposed the passage of the laws. But wherever herd laws were passed, the landscape—whether urban or rural—was much improved: village beautification organizations planted trees and vines on the margins of redeemed roads, urban fences disappeared, front lawns reached down to the street, and flowers bloomed in parks and graveyards and in front of houses.

Beginning in the 1860s, additional developments in the American countryside also indicated less reliance on fences and a tendency to reduce their number. Interior fences in many farms were taken down to create larger fields to accommodate the new farm machinery; in some cases, it was found that a single unfenced field was sufficient for certain types of crops. Moreover, groups of farmers sometimes cooperated to produce a single surrounding fence, thus greatly

When one has roamed, as I have, over those boundless and woodless prairies, extending thousands of miles away to the west, and south of us, the question of almost painful

reducing the cost of building fences. The town of Greeley, Colorado, solved the problem of stray livestock by building a large fence which enclosed the entire community—gardens, suburbs, neighboring small farms, and all.

Although reduced in number, fences were still needed and used in many parts of the West by farmers who raised cattle and grew crops. Wood, however, was expensive and often hard to find. Horticulturists and nurserymen promoted the use of hedges to keep out cattle. Hedges, however, had serious disadvantages: they took up room; discouraged growth near their roots; and unless regularly pruned and cared for, developed gaps and openings. So the search for a built fence that was durable, inexpensive, and easy to maintain continued throughout the Midwest. Hundreds of patents were issued for novel variations involving wire, vines, and even ditches.

The solution came in 1874 when Joseph Glidden of De Kalb, Illinois, produced a fence wire with many small barbs. The chronicle of that invention and its legal and commercial consequences has been written many times, which is not to minimize its revolutionary consequences. It had a major impact on the rural landscape and many aspects of agriculture. Nevertheless, for some years after its invention, barbed wire was still unknown in many parts of this country.

There were still areas where fences were of little importance—areas not yet settled and where the grazing of livestock on the open public range was the order of the day. Much of Texas, Kansas, and what is now Oklahoma, Colorado, and New Mexico, were part of what W.P. Webb has called the Cattle Kingdom.

The Cattle Kingdom was a vast, open, unpopulated region with scant rainfall, little surface water, and an immense undulating treeless landscape. For the most part, the area was covered by a dense growth of short grass, which needed little rain, constantly renewed itself, and was ideally suited to the raising of livestock. It was here, west of the 98th meridian (which runs roughly from northeastern North Dakota through the heart of Kansas down to the southernmost tip of Texas), that a very different kind of agriculture and cultural life had gradually evolved. It was similar in many respects to the cattle-oriented culture of Virginia and earlier Spanish and Mexican ranch culture. We have tended to idealize that cowboy culture; it had its picturesque and heroic aspects, but it did not last,

TOP
Pennington County,
South Dakota, 1936

ABOVE
Branding cattle, Utah

QUOTATION
Horace Capron, *Illinois State Agricultural Society Transactions* (1856-1857)

interest arises, how are these vast plains to be peopled? How are they to be tamed, subdued, and brought into proper use and cultivation? How are they to be FENCED?

TOP
Barbed-wire
advertisement

ABOVE
Barbed-wire
salesmen, Columbia
Patent Company,
Chicago, 1891

Left to right, standing: *Peter J.
McManus, George F. Rummel,
Ralph Eastman, James P. Tufts,
R.D. Carver, Getty Stewart,
Thomas F. Farmer.*
Seated: *Emery T. Ambler, Leroy
W. Garoutte, Charles Eastman,
J.T. McDonald, W.D. Ellsworth,
Peter H. Talley, J.D. Maher*

and it was in large part because of the introduction of the barbed-wire fence that it vanished.

Webb, the greatest writer on the Cattle Kingdom, briefly sketched the pre-barbed-wire landscape of the region and how it evolved: the practice of raising cattle on a large scale is *ranching*, and the owner of a ranch is a *ranchman* or *cattleman*. The ranchman typically selected the site for his ranch near grass and water. He established his home and headquarters near a stream, and his cattle grazed on the surrounding grass slopes. He had no neighbors and saw no need for fences of any kind. After a few years, other ranchers moved in, though they were fifteen or twenty miles away. They, too, grazed their cattle on the surrounding grassland and used the same stream, though both parties tacitly recognized a division between their two domains. Even so, the two herds commingled, and the only way of distinguishing them was by their brand. Twice a year there was a roundup, and the cowboys sorted out the different brands and collected their own. Eventually the rancher drove part of his herd across country to market them or ship them. It was a rough, monotonous, and even brutal existence, but it had its pleasures and excitements, most of them related to riding, roping, herding, and branding. Webb's glimpse brings back an earlier, more primitive Texas—one without roads or towns or cultivated fields or even houses: Texas before barbed wire and railroads, a marvelous windblown sea of grass.

That idyllic, rural Texas was the target of the promoters of Glidden wire. By the 1880s, the state had fully recovered from the war and represented a promising market for ranchers and farmers. Sanborn, the young partner of Glidden, had novel ideas about how to introduce the new wire. He built a barbed-wire corral in downtown San Antonio, filled it with half-wild longhorns, and invited the public to watch. Harassed by blazing torches, the animals made a mad rush into the fence and then retreated in dismay. Another rush ensued, and still the fence held—not only held, but bloodied many of the frantic animals. The public was frightened, then reassured, and Glidden barbed wire was welcomed.

One year later, Sanborn managed to acquire a total of 250,000 acres of empty rangeland in a remote part of the state. He enclosed the land with 150 miles of Glidden barbed wire, filled it with some fifteen hundred head of cattle, and invited the attention of the local cattlemen. The Flying Pan Ranch—named after the shape of Sanborn's brand—was the first, and for a long time the largest, enclosed ranch in Texas. Sanborn, however, had no intention of operating the new mega-ranch; he merely wanted to demonstrate that Glidden wire could hold fifteen hundred head of cattle.

His third promotion involved the construction of many miles of what were called drift fences, long stretches of east-west fence designed to prevent cattle from slowly moving south to escape the winter cold. The individual fences were not joined—they merely overlapped—but few cattle managed to find the openings. It so happened that the winter of 1885-86 was one of the worst on record, a sequence of deadly blizzards. "The cattle moved south driven by the wind and snow, like gray ghosts with icicles hanging from their muzzles, eyes and ears, directly into the drift fences... They stood stacked together against the wire, without food, water, warmth, or shelter... At the storm's end bodies were found piled against the wire, standing stiffly upright." It was "the big die-up," where thousands of cattle perished along Panhandle drift fences.

There was an outcry of horror from the general public and from the ranchers as well, for they felt responsible. They had personally witnessed the storm and had suffered large financial losses, but they suffered emotionally as well. At a time like the present when it is politically correct to revile all ranchers, it is well to bear in mind that many of them felt something like affection for the animals they had undertaken to feed and protect, and in fact, the most vocal objections to barbed-wire fence (which originally contained barbs one inch long) came from those ranchers whose cattle had been cruelly cut by the new style of fence.

The drama of the rise and fall of the Cattle Kingdom is best illustrated by the conflict in Texas between the proponents of "free grass" and those who relied on

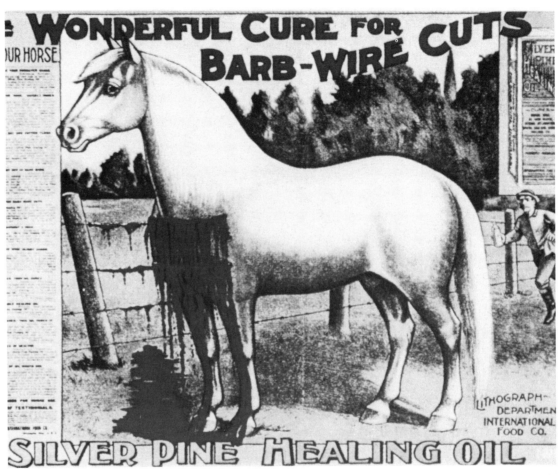

Advertisement for healing oil

Good and secure fences are better than a hot toddy, or all the soporific drugs of Turkey or Arabia, to sleep upon; you not only know where your cattle are, but where they are not.

Rural New Yorker (1856)

fencing. Throughout the whole semi-arid region west of the 98th meridian, the conflict followed the same course, with much the same outcome: the transformation of ranching into what Webb calls fenced stock farming and the opening up of the Great Plains to the small farmer. It is an extremely complicated story, and both sides in the conflict have eloquent advocates to this day. What concerns us is the role of barbed wire.

Many of the evil consequences of that conflict can be ascribed to the men who authorized the use of barbed wire. These powerful and well-established ranchers, in their determination to control the land, fenced up water holes which farmers and smaller ranchers needed, stretched wire across well-traveled roads, and prevented access to large areas of public lands by enclosing them with fences. Their fences often obliterated trails which cattle had been using for generations, and their continued construction of drift fences caused many more deaths. But barbed wire had its own destructive capacity: the strands used in the earliest barbed-wire fences were so small as to be invisible, and cattle were impaled, even when grazing in fenced areas. The fearsome barbs were another example of the lethal nature of the wire, and once again the ranchers spoke out and their indignation resulted in the production of a more visible type of wire, as well as laws banning the so-called "vicious" wire.

The old-fashioned fences of rails or boards had not only been highly visible to cattle and entirely harmless, they had also taken time to build and had gradually become a familiar element in the topography of the field. There were a few instances, even during the heyday of the barbed-wire fence, of ranchers who experimented with using trees and bushes as fences. They confined the cattle very successfully and produced an ecosystem to which the animals seemed to respond. The barbed-wire fence, visible or "vicious," remained an alien element, an intruder, totally unrelated to the enclosed elements, both human and animal. That is why the barbed-wire fence was so easy to remove, psychologically as well as physically, and why it was so rarely tolerated as part of the domestic landscape.

Its greatest shortcoming, however, was that it was used and perceived not as a means of creating a unique space, but as a means of controlling movement, by impeding or channeling it in one direction. The fence cutters active in the 1880s were not content with destroying the restraining strands of fence; they often deliberately twisted and tangled the remaining lengths of wire, allowing the two spaces to merge. The barbed-wire fence was most effective when it eliminated *existing* spaces by dividing them with a rigid, unnatural barrier, by closing roads, and by discouraging gates and openings. If we lament the disappearance of the old "romantic" ranch culture, we can blame the visual affront of the long, monotonous perspective of straight vertical posts in a landscape of undulating horizontal forms.

The farms which invaded the High Plains in the late nineteenth century rarely had interior fences, and the only fences we see now are those erected along roads by the highway departments—to channel traffic and fragment the landscape. Our landscape is a palimpsest of an infinite number of schemes for organizing space to produce a sense of security and freedom. If the high-tech arrogance symbolized by the barbed-wire fence is in truth on its way out, why should we not look forward to a new landscape where the fence once more celebrates and dignifies its content?

The fence and the boundary line are the symbols of the spirit of justice. They set the limits upon each man's interest to prevent one from taking advantage of the other.

Reinhold Niebuhr, *The Nature and Destiny of Man* (1943)

Fence cutters,
reenactment,
Nebraska, 1885

Iowa farmstead, 1942

WIRED! THE FENCE INDUSTRY AND THE INVENTION OF CHAIN LINK

Gregory K. Dreicer

Chain-link fence weaves through our lives, subdividing the land, cutting our views of city and country into facets. The steely mesh of the chain link fence has become a natural part of our world. Although it has skirted backyards, factories, and playgrounds for one hundred years, we know little about its origins. This essay traces the history of wire fence, from smooth to barbed, from woven to chain link.

The preoccupation with fences began building in North America when Europeans established their first communities. It continued to grow during the second half of the nineteenth century, as farmers tripled their acreage, ironworkers erected skyscraping cities, and trackmen laid a vast network of rail. This rural and urban building boom intensified the quest for a reliable fence that could be manufactured, delivered, and built cheaply, quickly, and on a mass scale.

At that time, iron and steel were gradually replacing stone and wood in many products, including bridges, boats, and hand tools. Metal is not superior to wood, but it possesses characteristics that make it irresistible to industrial designers. Its availability as a raw material, as well as its mutable composition and form, mean that it is suitable for relatively lightweight mass-produced products that must endure heavy and repeated stress.

Wire is created by pulling a heated, lubricated metal rod through a series of perforated metal plates; the sizes of the holes in the plates determines the thickness of the wire. The metal strand can be bent, spun, and woven into

OPPOSITE PAGE
Workers and wire coils at American Steel & Wire Company, Worcester, Massachusetts, ca. 1934

ABOVE
South Bartonville Works, Keystone Steel & Wire Company, Peoria, Illinois, 1920

Product label,
Washburn & Moen
Manufacturing
Company

Wire netting,
Brockner & Evans
advertisement

frameworks, cables, and textiles. During the 1830s and 1840s, technologists in industrializing countries such as England, Belgium, Germany, and the United States mechanized manufacturing methods while increasing wire's strength and elasticity. Techniques introduced during the 1870s allowed the industrial production of steel of uniform quality. The Washburn & Moen Manufacturing Company of Worcester, Massachusetts, however, had struck gold with steel wire during the previous decade, when they produced about three hundred tons annually, just for hoop skirts.[1] This fashion was only one of the ways that steel wire insinuated itself into our lives. From corsets to paper clips, dental tools to piano strings, dish racks to suspension bridges, we hang from wire and wire hangs from us.

Farmers, government officials, and editors of agricultural journals commented anxiously during the nineteenth century on the increasing lack of timber as well as the heavy financial burden of fence construction. Wire was sometimes suggested as an alternative, and indeed, rudimentary wire fences—several wires stretched taut between posts or trees—were increasingly common after the mid-nineteenth century. It is estimated that 350,000 miles of galvanized wire was used for fences between 1850 and 1870.[2] For example, John Nesmith of Lowell, Massachusetts, received a patent in 1854 for a fence-making machine, and the next year the Lowell Wire Fence Company advertised in agricultural journals throughout the United States. Wire became a familiar sight, hanging between poles as part of the expanding telegraph network, as netting for windows and chicken coops, and in the ornamental fences chosen by home owners. By 1874, an inventor noted that "wire fences [were] in common use," although it was not generally accepted by agricultural and industry as a reliable fence material: livestock "contentedly sawed their itching necks... on the smooth wire, in the acme of creature satisfac-tion, until the fence gave way."[3]

In 1872, the Commissioner of the United States Department of Agriculture deemed "the fence debt a heavier burden than the war debt" when he announced that the value of fences enclosing the 250,505,614 acres of the thirty-seven United States totaled $1,747,549,091. He declared "the cost of fence [maintenance] nearly equal to the total amount of the national debt on which interest is paid, and about the same as the estimated value of all the farm animals in the United States."[4] These figures did not include residential and commercial fences. The U.S.D.A. Commissioner's report appeared approximately two years before farmers and ranchers began to string barbed wire across the American continent, replacing the zigzag wooden rails of the worm fence with a tracery of steel wire.

The genius of wire designs such as the safety pin and the chain-link fence is found not only in their physical structure and appearance, but in the way they are produced. The crux of fence development, and the history of the industrialization of construction in general, lies in the ability to make and assemble products on a mass scale. As the United States expanded and industrialized, fences became a focus of invention. Between 1801 and 1857, inventors registered one hundred fence patents; from 1866 to 1868, there were an additional 368; and by 1881 there were 1229 patents relating to fences.[5] Inventors who devised methods of producing fences quickly and cheaply could become rich.

Joseph F. Glidden's barbed wire patent of November 24, 1874, demonstrated that enormous profits could be made from industrialized wire fence. Previous patents had included wire strands, wire barbs, and combinations of the two; Glidden's patent described a wire barb coiled into a double strand of twisted wire so that the barb would remain fixed against thrusting cattle. Glidden became partners

That Iowa's tillable lands can not be fenced off in eighty acre fields, by cutting down every stick of wood fit at all for the purpose, is not a subject of argument, it is a matter of the five senses. Nobody denies it; everybody admits that "sometime or other something must be done." Yet this being a "disagreeable" subject, and every one being busy with fixing for himself a little spot of this great "unmade garden," we continue the practice against our better impulses of the principle "after me the deluge." We destroy grove after grove [by cutting trees for fence wood], and leave the future to take care of itself. Yet that dreaded future is coming upon us closer with every season; in fact it is already upon us. Our present needs of fencing material are ahead of our supplies. This is a matter of every day experience with very many Iowa Farmers; and has stimulated them to very earnest and systematic efforts to find a substitute.

From "What Shall We Do For Fences?" by Fred Summerschu, Iowa State Agricultural Society, *Annual Report* 7 (1860).

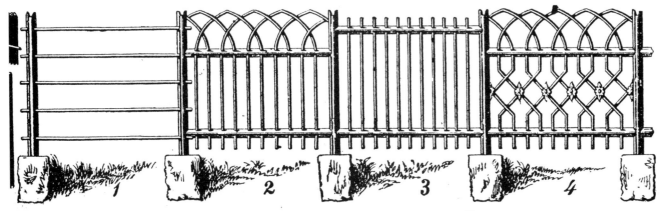

Wire fences, New York Wire Railing Company catalog, 1857

Calendar illustration,
1901

with businessman Isaac L. Ellwood and then sold his share to wire manufacturers Washburn & Moen, who employed mechanics to develop automatic machinery. Their purchase of almost all related patents ensured these manufacturers enormous profits. Ellwood and people such as inventor Jacob Haish made DeKalb, Illinois, the center of the barbed-wire industry. Ellwood's residence, now a museum, stands as a monument to their success.[6]

The fence industry typified the turn-of-the-century transformation of small trade into vertically integrated big business: fence producers became part of larger firms that included mines, raw-material production plants, and transportation facilities. Barbed- and woven-wire fence, along with wire nails, were basic products behind the industrial consolidation that resulted in the formation of the American Steel and Wire Company, which by 1899 had a monopoly on barbed wire. In 1901, this firm became a subsidiary of the United States Steel Corporation (now USX), which annually produced more than seventy-five percent of wire rod in the United States during the first decade of the twentieth century. It was also one of the firms that sparked the antitrust movement.[7]

Dissatisfaction with barbed wire, which pierced the valuable hides of livestock as well as the soft skin of human hands, led states to pass legislation against its use and encouraged technologists to develop a fence of barbless woven wire.[8] But farmers, who should have been the most avid consumers of the woven product, were wary. They had gained a poor impression from earlier fences of cheap wire.[9] Fence building was not a simple task; it involved a significant investment of time, labor, and money. Farmers had to dig holes, install posts, and mount and stretch the wire so that it would not yield to livestock or sag in the heat; in addition, they had to maintain the fence. Farmers had reason for caution: defective wire could jeopardize their investment and result in devastating losses if crops were destroyed when a fence failed to keep animals in or out.

The power of smooth woven wire was demonstrated at county fairs as well as in Madison Square Garden in New York City, where it was reported circa 1890 that "a big dude one day thrust a red silk umbrella through the fence directly into the face of Grover, a mammoth bull buffalo, who instantly lunged at his tormentor" but did not maul him, thanks to the woven-wire fence. According to Arthur W. Sprague, an employee of Ellwood, it was "almost impossible" to sell Ellwood woven fence between 1895 and 1897 because farmers did not believe that it was durable. Ellwood hired salesmen in Ohio and Michigan who erected fence for farmers free-of-charge just to prove its effectiveness. Later, when Sprague became head of sales at American Steel and Wire, production went from 15,156 tons of woven-wire fence during the last nine months of 1898 to 107,098 tons in 1902 to 303,461 in 1912. In 1906, a manufacturer estimated that eighty percent of hardware stores in the West carried woven-wire fence as standard stock.[10]

The development of fence-weaving machinery is not easily traced. Wire industry veteran Kenneth B. Lewis reported that industrial competition in the United States meant that fence "weaving machines... designed and built in the users' plants [are] about as easy to get hold of as the owner's right eye."[11] Woven wire, which was more difficult to manufacture than barbed wire, came to occupy people such as J. Wallace Page, who like many fence technologists was born on a farm and lived near the edge of the expanding fence-starved frontier. Page experimented with stakes and wire. In May 1883, he erected a hand-woven fence between his farm and the farm of his neighbors the Cook Brothers. The fence was made of thirteen horizontal wires with vertical wires one foot apart. Page's cousin, Charles M. Lamb, who developed many patentable ideas for the Page Woven Wire Fence Company, transformed the hand loom into a power loom in 1888. Meanwhile, William Bell of Verona, Mississippi, had patented a prototypic square-mesh woven-wire field fence in 1886, but he lacked a design for a power loom and never produced the fence on a large scale.[12] Between 1886 and 1890, Herman Schnabel of Chicago worked on a machine that produced woven-wire fence for the Ellwood Manufacturing Company. He developed a preliminary device for a fence with a diamond-shaped mesh.

Around 1892, Albert J. Bates of Joliet, Illinois, further developed Schnabel's work. He studied the Frost Wire Fence Company's product, made of crimped wire—to prevent sagging and stretching—as well as the square mesh of Page and the

Wire-fence entrepreneur
Isaac L. Ellwood

Barbed-wire machine
and wooden spools of
barbed wire, early
twentieth century

ABOVE
Early fence experiment
of J. Wallace Page

OPPOSITE PAGE
Crimped wire fence,
Grundy County,
Iowa, 1940

diamond mesh of Keystone Steel & Wire of Peoria, Illinois, which was founded in 1889 and continues to manufacture many types of wire fence. Inspired, Bates then created American Square Mesh Fencing.[13] The wire-fence machines he patented in 1896 and 1897 made possible rapid, inexpensive production of large quantities of fence. He wrote in a letter to the Commissoner of Patents that his "greatest object [was] to produce fencing... more cheaply than [has] heretofore been done."[14] In his machine, short vertical wires connected the long horizontal wires, and many vertical wires could be fed and coiled at once, thereby multiplying production capability. But Bates was only one of several woven-wire pioneers. J. Wallace Page, for example, widely advertised the fence made at his factory in Adrian, Michigan. He integrated vertically by building a wire plant to supply the factory and a steel mill to supply the plant. Others, inspired by demonstrations at the 1893 World's Columbian Exposition in Chicago, created electrically welded fence.[15]

It must be noted that without posts a wire fence cannot stand. During the final decades of the last century, steel posts joined wooden posts as the fence builder's stock-in-trade. Although one of the first barbed-wire inventors included a cast-iron post in his scheme, the development of metal posts took a number of years and commanded the attention of many technologists. A superior post would be made of a small amount of metal and would be rapidly produced; it would not rust in the ground, would not be heaved by frost, and would resist the tension put into wire fence, as well as the onslaught of raging bulls. The patents of Philip J. Harrah of Bloomfield, Indiana, one of the fathers of the galvanized steel fence post, were purchased in 1911 by the American Steel and Wire Company. The next year, the firm produced ten thousand tons of posts with improved machinery. The year after, it doubled its output, producing 5,600,000 tubular steel posts.[16]

Prior to the introduction of chain link, which is reported to have been devised in Germany around 1859, fences of woven wire were sometimes fortified by two or three strands of smooth wire threaded from post to post through the fence mesh.[17] Chain link, with its thicker interlocking wires, did not need such reinforcing. It is made up of a series of vertical wires, each of which is bent into a zigzag before being inserted into an identically angular neighbor. A series of these zigzags constitutes a chain of linked wires that appears to be a woven fabric of diagonal wires. It is not woven, however, because there is a warp but no woof; that is, only vertical wires are used.

Fig. 1.

B ... A
e b c
C ... A
C
B ... E
a ... a
C ... D ... E
D ... C ... E
B ... D ... E
C ... D ... E
B ... D ... E

Fig. 1.   Fig. 2.

Fig. 3.   Fig. 4.   Fig. 5.   Fig. 6.

Diamond Lawn Fence
2-INCH MESH
Made in Six Heights and Three Styles.   Furnished in 10 and 20 Rod Rolls.
(Non-Climbable)

Heights:
58-in.
50-in.
42-in.
34-in.
26-in.
18-in.

4" 4" 2"

Actual size of Wire as follows: Specifications I   Specifications J   Specifications K

Horizontal Cables No. 12½   No. 12½   No. 12½

Cross Wires.......No. 14   No. 12½   No. 12½

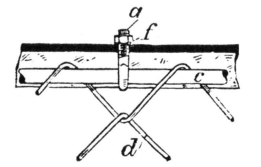

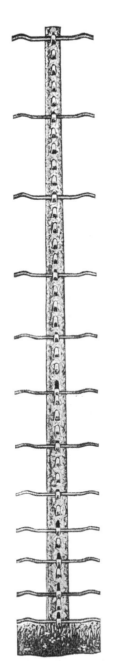

Fence post, American
Steel & Wire Company,
1913

Wire fence, Lamb Fence
Company, ca. 1900

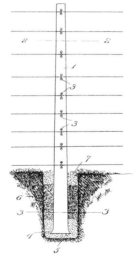

Philip J. Harrah's fence
post, patent drawing,
1906

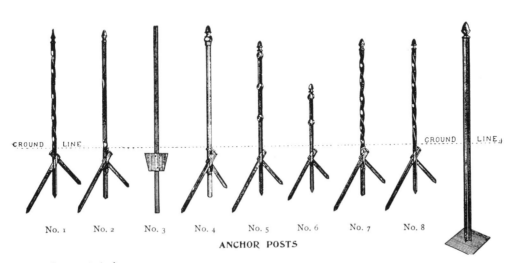

GROUND LINE   GROUND LINE

No. 1   No. 2   No. 3   No. 4   No. 5   No. 6   No. 7   No. 8

ANCHOR POSTS

Fence posts, Anchor
Post Iron Works

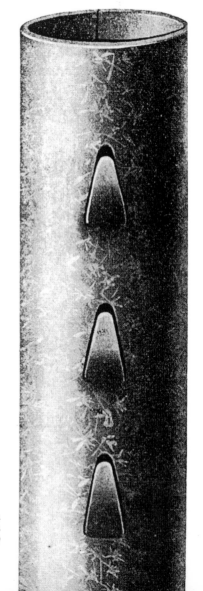

Fence post, American
Steel & Wire Company,
1929

An early type of chain-link machine was a hand-cranked device that bent individual wires. The craftsperson then took each zigzag wire, threaded it into the next, and twisted their top and bottom ends together. Chain link would not be sold in large quantity, however, until mechanics developed machinery that could perform these tasks rapidly and continuously. In Pfullingen, Germany, in 1893, Ernst Wagner built such a machine and established a factory; further improvements were made by Otto Schmid of Feuerbach, Germany, between 1906 and 1909. Competitors Wagner and Schmid united in 1914 to form what today is known as the Wafios Machinery Corporation of Reutlingen, Germany.[18] The chain-link machine bends the wire as it spirals it into a wire it has already bent. It then cuts the wire, determining the height of the fence; twists together the ends of each pair of wires; and winds the resulting fabric into a roll suitable for shipping.

When, where, and how did chain link arrive in North America? Page Two, Inc. of Bartonville, Illinois, a firm which traces itself back to J. Wallace Page, reports that during the 1880s an inventor named Jacob Schneider imported a chain-link loom he had developed "in Switzerland." John, Samuel, and Timotheus Hohulin, of Goodfield, Illinois, who ran a hardware store, acquired the machine and received their first order in 1897, for a fence that was 396 feet long and forty-eight inches high. Ten years later, they decided to concentrate solely on the production of chain link, which they supplied to several other companies, including Stewart Iron Works of Covington, Kentucky, which today manufactures ornamental metal fences, and the Cyclone Fence Company of Waukegan, Illinois. A Hohulin Brothers catalog published circa 1915 shows several styles of "diamond link wire fence," including what they called "our 1906 iron post yard fence." They stated that it had "met with success far beyond our expectations."[19]

Around the turn of the century, several inventors in the United States patented fence posts, fence-making machines, and portable-fence systems that included chain link, but they did patent the chain link itself, nor did they use the term "chain link."[20] The Hohulin Brothers' 1904 fence-post patent (they filed the application in 1901) shows what appears to be chain-link fabric stretched between posts. A surviving Hohulin order book seems to indicate that fences of this type were installed during 1905; one of these venerable structures still stands in Goodfield, Illinois.

The Anchor Group of Baltimore, Maryland, reports that at a 1906 sales meeting of the Anchor Post Iron Works of Garwood, New Jersey, incorporated in

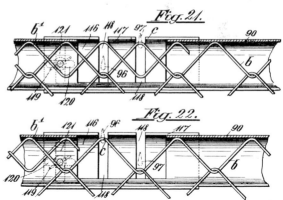

OPPOSITE PAGE
Chain-link machines, Reeves Southeastern Corporation, Tampa, Florida, ca. 1965

TOP
Chain link, The Stewart Iron Works Company catalog

ABOVE
Manufacture of chain link, as shown in Otto Schmid's patent drawing, 1911

1892, a discussion was held concerning a fence fabric made on a hand loom "that one Jacob Schneider living in Rockville, Connecticut had brought with him from Belgium." Anchor Post eventually purchased the patents and went to work improving them.[21] The January 30, 1908, issue of the trade journal *Iron Age* presented one of the earliest published descriptions in the U.S. of "chain link wire fence." The next year, *Sweets Catalog*, a source book for the building industry, printed under the heading "fences for factories, mills, and industrial properties" an Anchor Post advertisement that showed an eight-foot tall, 3,500-foot long, chain-link fence installed at the Crocker-Wheeler Company in Ampere, New Jersey. (Crocker-Wheeler manufactured electric equipment such as motors, generators, and transformers.) During the second decade of the century, chain link appeared in the trade catalogs of firms such as the F.E. Carpenter Company and J.W. Fiske Iron Works, both of New York, and the W.A. Snow Iron Works of Boston.[22]

During the 1930s, Wafios exported chain-link machinery to U.S. companies such as Wright Wire of Worcester, Massachusetts. On the west coast, Frank Bergandi, an immigrant from Italy, who was familiar with the German equipment, built chain-link machines, assisted by Herbert Rohrbacher. Bergandi Manufac-turing was established in the Los Angeles area; by the 1960s it had become a wire mill that produced machines upon request. Today, Bergandi Machinery Company is the sole producer of chain-link machines in the U.S. Its competitors are based in Germany, Italy, and Japan.[23]

While crops and cattle provided the impetus for the development of barbed and woven wire, the initial rise of chain link is probably tied to military security as well as an army of new home owners. War played a pivotal role in the development of many of the technologies we take for granted; the security requirements of both World Wars accelerated chain link production as it hastened the demise of woven wire fence, which was melted for scrap. Fences needed for postwar residential and industrial building gave a further boost to chain link.[24]

The 1993 residential market for fence manufacture and installation was estimated to be worth about $3 billion; if commercial use were included, that number would be twice as large. Of the 72,000 miles of residential fence produced, about fifty-four percent was chain link.[25] That's enough to encircle the earth three times. Polyvinyl chloride (plastic) fence is gaining in popularity, but for years to come, America will remain wired.

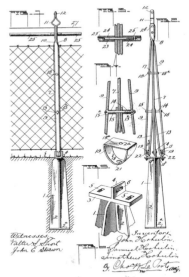

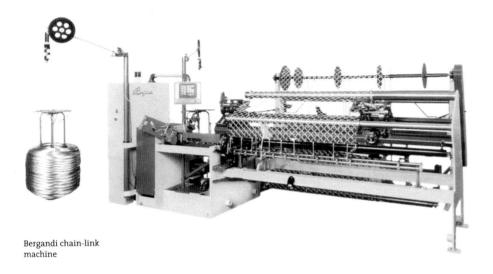

Bergandi chain-link machine

TOP
Chain link, Hohulin Brother's fence-post patent drawing, 1904

ABOVE
Hohulin Brothers' chain-link fence, Goodfield, Illinois, 1996

1. Peter Temin, *Iron and Steel in Nineteenth-Century America: An Economic Inquiry* (Cambridge: MIT Press, 1964), 125-45; "History of Worcester Works," probably written by Charles R. Sturtevant , ca. 1907 in American Steel and Wire Company Collection, Baker Library, Harvard University, Dcc-549. (Hereafter referred to as ASW Collection); "The Washburn Wire Works," in J. Leander Bishop, *History of American Manufactures from 1608 to 1860* (Philadelphia: E. Young & Co., 1868), 344-47.

2. *DeKalb County Manufacturer* (1882), 4, reprinted by Charles C. Hunt, ed. (DeKalb, Ill., 1972). See Clarence H. Danhof, "The Fencing Problem in the Eighteen-Fifties," *Agricultural History* 18 (1944): 184-86; *The Plough, The Loom and the Anvil* (1849): 177-79, in *Memoirs of Philadelphia Agricultural Society*, "Account of Wire Fences by White & Hazard (Jan. 8, 1816); Edward Clark, "Fences," from *Annual Report of American Institute*, N.Y.C., in *Transactions of New York State Agricultural Society* 5 (1845): 516.

3. Danhof, 185; ASW Collection, MS 596 A512B, G.L. Meaker and L.C. Bailey, "History of the Manfuacture of Poultry Netting and Meshed Fabric" (American Steel and Wire Company of New Jersey, 1913), 3-4; Kathleen Randall, "Early Wire Fences," *Old House Journal* 20 (March 1992): 28, 30; inventor Charles Kennedy, U.S. Patent 153, 965, 11 August 1874; *DeKalb County Manufacturer* (1882), 4.

4. Annual maintenance was estimated at $93,963,187 plus six percent interest ($104,852,995, based on total value), to total $198,806,182. U.S.D.A., *Report of the Commissioner of Agriculture for the Year 1871* (Washington: Government Printing Office, 1872), 509-11.

5. ASW Collection, Dce-1206, Charles G. Washburn, "Barbed Fencing," 2.

6. Henry D. and Frances T. McCallum, *Wire that Fenced the West* (Norman, Okla., University of Oklahoma Press, 1965), 46; ASW Collection, Case 3, Washburn & Moen, Dcc-872, "Decision of U.S. Supreme Court by Judge Brown [1891]," 8; Joseph M. McFadden, "Monopoly in Barbed Wire: The Formation of the American Steel and Wire Company," *Business History Review* 52 (1978): 465-89.

7. McFadden, 465-89; Alfred D. Chandler, Jr., *The Visible Hand: Mangerial Revolution in American Business* (Cambridge, Mass.: Harvard University Press, 1977), 359-63; "Vitality of the Wire Industry," *Iron Age* 86 (1910): 744-45.

8. "History of the Manufacture of Woven Wire Fencing," 1; ASW Collection, Dcf-352, MS 596, "Fencing" /1875 1935/A512/Box 9, "Transcript of Record: Denning Wire & Fence Co. vs. American Steel & Wire Co.," 9 March 1907; Earl W. Hayter, "The Fencing of Western Railways," *Agricultural History* 19 (1945): 165; Earl W. Hayter, "Barbed Wire Fencing—A Prairie Invention," *Agricultural History* 13 (1939): 193-94.

9. Horace Capron, "Wire Fences," *Transactions of Illinois State Agricultural Society* 2 (1856-57): 427-28; "History of the Manufacture of Woven Wire Fencing," 8-9. Advertising brochure *Treatise on Wire Fencing* (Boston: James E. Butts, Jr. & Co., 1856) cites positive press commentary. Woven-wire fence should be corrosion-resistant and have adequately-spaced wires with reliable connections; see Walter M. Floto, "Problems in the Production of Farm Fencing," *Agricultural Engineering* 16 (1935): 480.

10. "History of the Manufacture of Woven Wire Fencing," 8, 54-58; "Wire Fencing," *Iron Age* (12 July 1906): 120.

11. Kenneth B. Lewis, *Steel Wire in America* (Stamford, Conn.: Wire Assoc., 1952), 341.

12. ASW Collection, MS 596 A512C, G.L. Meaker and L.C. Bailey, "History of the Manufacture of Woven Wire Fencing" (American Steel and Wire Company of New Jersey, 1913), 3-6. For history of Page Steel and Wire Co., see "ACCO and Fencing—A Long Partnership," *Wire Technology* 5, no. 2 (1977); Beryle G. Sweet, "A Brief History of Page Aluminized Steel Corporation and Page Two Inc.," typescript, n.d.

13. ASW Collection, Dcc-908, letter from Brown Fence & Wire, 19 Oct. 1911, and letter from Frost Wire, 21 Oct. 1911, both to American Steel and Wire.

14. National Archives, Albert J. Bates to Commissioner of Patents, 24 Feb. 1896, U.S. Patent File 561,193.

15. "History of the Manufacture of Woven Wire Fencing," 3-10, 49. For a description of manufacturing processes, see J.L. Schueler, "The Engineering Side of Producing Woven Wire Fencing," *Agricultural Engineering* 15 (1934): 391-93.

16. ASW Collection, c. 7, Dcc-910, A.W. Sprague, "Story of the American Steel Fence Post," 1913. The early barbed wire inventor was Lucien B. Smith, U.S. Patent 66, 182, 25 June 1867.

17. The date, 1859, provided by "A Brief History of Chain Link Fence," Chain Link Fence Manufacturers Institute, Washington, D.C., n.d.

18. Werner Neubrander, "Vortrag beim Reutlinger Industriemuseum, 7 April 1995, Wafios Maschinenfabrik GmbH, Reutlingen, Germany; Otto Schmid, U.S. Patent 1,005,480 (10 Oct. 1911).

19. "Original Wire Weaving Machine Links Hohulin's 80-Year History," Page Two, Inc., Bartonville, Ill., n.d.; "The Hohulin Family: 64 Years of Fencing," *Fence Industry Trade News* 4 (July 1961): 16-18; Hohulin Bros., Goodfield, Ill., *The Diamond Link Wire Fence* , Cat. no. 12, [ca. 1915], 12-13; ASW Collection, Dcg-310, "History of Cyclone Fence Company," Cyclone Fence Co, Chicago, [Jan. 1926], 7.

20. See J.W. Le Gore, U.S. Patent 616,545 (27 Dec. 1898); J.,S., and T. Hohulin, U.S. Patent 764,468 (5 July 1904); O. Tuerke, U.S. Patent 803,941 (7 Nov. 1905); J.,S., and T. Hohulin, U.S. Patent 871, 698 (19 Nov. 1907); A. Schneider, U.S. Patent 1,014,525 (9 Jan 1912).

21. "Sales Manual—Fence Division: Background Notes," Anchor Group, Baltimore, Md., n.d.

22. Catalogs in the collections of Avery Library, Columbia University, and Library of Congress. According to ASW Collection, Dcg-310, "History of Cyclone Fence Company," Cyclone Fence Co, Chicago, [Jan. 1926], 7, a chain-link fence machine and salesman were shipped from Germany to New York City in 1914. After about five months without success, and one week before the outbreak of World War I, the salesman sold the machine to Cyclone, which had two additional looms built based on the original model and sold these to firms in Canada and South Africa.

23. Walter Knapp, "100 Year Odyssey," Worcester Historical Museum, 10; Personal communication with Marcie T. Rohrbacher, President, Bergandi Machinery Co., 19 January 1996; Paul C. Harder, "High Speed Fabric Weaver: History and Development by a Mechanical Genius," *Fence Industry* (August 1959): 16-18.

24. Donald Albrecht, ed., *World War II and the American Dream: How Wartime Building Changed a Nation* (Washington, D.C.: National Building Museum/MIT Press, 1995); "History of Cyclone Fence Company," 7-8; Randall, 30.

25. 44% was wood; 2% was ornamental metals and plastic. Estimated figures provided by Terry Dempsey, Executive Vice President, American Fence Association.

Installing chain link,
Busch Gardens,
Tampa, Florida

CONTRIBUTORS

DIANA BALMORI is founder and Principal for Design of Balmori Associates, Inc. of New Haven. She holds a joint appointment with the Yale University Schools of Architecture and of Forestry and Environmental Studies. Her publications include *Saarinen House and Garden* (1995), *Redesigning the American Lawn* (1993), and *Transitory Gardens, Uprooted Lives* (1993).

ESTELLA M. CHUNG is a recent graduate of the University of Michigan in Ann Arbor, where she specialized in American culture. She served as assistant for the *Between Fences* catalog and exhibition.

PHILIP DOLE is Professor of Architecture Emeritus at the University of Oregon in Eugene, where he has taught since 1956. Dole's publications include *The Picket Fence in Oregon: An American Vernacular Comes West* (1986).

GREGORY K. DREICER is a curator at the National Building Museum. He is an historian of technology who specializes in modern building. Dreicer's exhibitions include *Barn Again!* (1994) and his articles have appeared in *Culture Technique* and *History and Technology*.

JOHN BRINCKERHOFF JACKSON is an historian of the American landscape. Now retired, he has taught at various institutions, including Harvard University and the University of California in Berkeley. Jackson was founder of *Landscape* magazine, which he edited for seventeen years. His publications include *American Space* (1972), *Discovering the Vernacular Landscape* (1984), and *A Sense of Place, A Sense of Time* (1994).

MAGGIE KELLY, editor of this catalog, is an architectural historian and Acting Curator of Architecture at the Chicago Historical Society. Her exhibitions include *From Bauhaus to Your House: Modernism and the Chicago Home* (1995) and *The Drawings of Harry Weese* (1995).

GARY KULIK is an historian, curator, and museum professional. He is Deputy Director for the Library and Academic Programs at Winterthur Museum, Garden, and Library. His publications include *The New England Mill Village, 1790-1800* (1980).

ANNE M. LANGE, Adjunct Assistant Professor, teaches literature and communications at Pace University, Pleasantville, New York, where she launched the Writing Laboratory. She is an antiquarian bookseller and her letters appear in the William Safire books *On Language* and *I Stand Corrected*.

J. ABBOTT MILLER is a designer and writer. He is director of Design/Writing/Research, based in New York City. He is the co-author, with Ellen Lupton, of *Design Writing Research: Writing on Graphic Design* (1996), *The Bathroom, The Kitchen, and The Aesthetics of Waste* (1992), and *The ABC's of ▲■●: The Bauhaus and Design Theory* (1991).

ANNE STILLMAN is consultant to the Connecticut Trust for Historic Preservation on land use and historic gardens. She is contributing editor of *Connecticut Preservation News* and editor of *Historic Properties Exchange*.

ILLUSTRATION CREDITS

COVER

*Security guard opening gate,
Buick plant, Melrose Park, Illinois, 1941*
Photograph by Ken Hedrich, Hedrich-
Blessing, courtesy Chicago Historical
Society, HB-06781-C.

FOREWORD

PAGE 6
The Stewart Iron Works Company,
Covington, Ky.

**FENCES AND THE SETTLEMENT
OF NEW ENGLAND**

PAGE 10
Theodor de Bry, *America* (Frankfurt,
1593), 70. Courtesy of the Library
of Congress, Prints and Photographs
Division

PAGE 11
From *Coastal New England: Its Life
and Past* by William F. Robinson,
copyright 1983 by William F.
Robinson. By permission of Little,
Brown, and Company

PAGE 12
Samuel de Champlain, *Les Voyages
de la Nouvelle France* (Paris: Claude
Collet, 1632) Rare Books and
Manuscripts Division, The New York
Public Library, Astor, Lenox and
Tilden Foundations.

PAGE 14
Courtesy of the Library of Congress,
Prints and Photographs Division

PAGE 15
Abner Reed, The Connecticut
Historical Society, Hartford,
Connecticut

PAGE 16
*Combination Atlas of Yates County
New York* (Philadelphia, 1876), 81.
Courtesy of the Library of Congress,
Geography and Maps Division

THE WORM FENCE

PAGE 18
Isaac Weld, *Travels thorough the
States of North America... during the
years 1795, 1796, and 1797* (London:
John Stockdale, 1800), 27. Courtesy,
The Winterthur Library: Printed Book
and Periodical Collection

PAGE 19
George A. Martin, *Fences, Gates, and
Bridges* (N.Y.: O. Judd Co., 1887;
reprint, Brattleboro, Vermont: Alan C.
Hood & Co., 1992), 9

PAGE 20
TOP: John Warner Barber, *Historical
collections... of every town in
Massachusetts* (Worcester: Dorr,
Howland, and Co., 1839), 269.
Courtesy, The Winterthur Library:
Printed Book and Periodical
Collection
ABOVE: Photograph by J.S. Cotton,
National Archives

PAGES 21-22
George A. Martin, *Fences, Gates, and
Bridges* (N.Y.: O. Judd Co., 1887;
reprint, Brattleboro, Vermont: Alan C.
Hood & Co., 1992), 8. Courtesy, The
Winterthur Library: Printed Book and
Periodical Collection

PAGE 21
*Luigi Castiglioni's Viaggio: Travels in
the United States of North America,
1785-87* (Syracuse: Syracuse
University Press, 1983). Courtesy, The
Winterthur Library: Printed Book and
Periodical Collection

PAGE 22
Photograph by M.E. Diemer, State
Historical Society of Wisconsin,
WHI(X3)28397

PAGE 23
George A. Martin, *Fences, Gates, and
Bridges* (N.Y.: O. Judd Co., 1887;
reprint, Brattleboro, Vermont: Alan C.
Hood & Co., 1992), 97

PAGE 24
TOP: Photograph by Dr. E.A. Bass,
State Historical Society of Wisconsin,
WHI B35 117
ABOVE: *Illustrated Atlas Map of
Sangamon County, Illinois* (Ill.: Brink,
McCormick and Co., 1874), 82.
Courtesy of the Library of Congress,
Geography and Maps Division

THE PICKET FENCE AT HOME

PAGE 26
Photograph courtesy of the Douglas
County Museum of History and
Natural History

PAGE 27
J.W. Barber, *Historical Collections
of the State of New York* (Worcester,
Mass., 1841)

PAGE 28
*Illustrated Atlas Map of Sangamon
County, Illinois* (Ill.: Brink, McCormick
and Co., 1874), 82. Courtesy of the
Library of Congress, Geography and
Maps Division

PAGE 29
Photograph by Lewis Wickens Hine,
Courtesy of the Library of Congress,
Prints and Photographs Division

PAGE 30
TOP: Oregon Historical Society,
ORH-28186
ABOVE: *Sloan's Victorian Buildings*
(N.Y.: Dover Pubs., 1990)

PAGE 31
TOP: Courtesy of Philip Dole
ABOVE: Photograph courtesy of the
Douglas County Museum of History
and Natural History

PAGE 32
TOP: Courtesy, Peabody Essex
Museum, Salem, Mass.
MIDDLE: Courtesy, The Bancroft
Library
BOTTOM: Oregon Historical Society,
ORH-38018

PAGE 33
A.T. Andreas, *Illustrated Atlas of the
State of Iowa* (Chicago: Andreas Atlas
Co., 1875), 169. Courtesy State
Historical Society of Iowa—Iowa City

PAGE 34
Special Collections Division,
University of Washington Special
Libraries, UW-10966

PAGE 35
Sketch by Private Schultz, Special
Collections Division, University
of Washington Special Libraries,
UW-9475

AMERICA FENCED

PAGE 36-37
Fence built in 1890, Ola, Idaho
Photograph by Dorothea Lange,
Library of Congress, Prints and
Photographs Division, FSA-OWI
Collection, LC-USF34-21606-C

PAGE 38
LEFT: *Cutting buckwheat, Nicholas
County, West Virginia, 1927*
Photograph by J.S. Cotton, National
Archives

RIGHT: *Ozark mountain farmer,
Missouri, 1940*
Photograph by John Vachon,
Library of Congress, Prints and
Photographs Division, FSA-OWI
Collection, LC-USF34-61046-D

PAGE 39
*Ranch fence, Beaverhead County,
Montana, 1942*
Photograph by Russell Lee, Library of
Congress, Prints and Photographs
Division, FSA-OWI Collection, LC-
USW3-8052-E

PAGE 40
LEFT: *School yard*
The Stewart Iron Works Company,
Covington, Ky.
RIGHT: *Playground*
The Stewart Iron Works Company,
Covington, Ky.

PAGE 41
Playground, Elwood Park, Illinois, 1955
Photograph by Bill Hedrich, Hedrich-
Blessing, courtesy Chicago Historical
Society, HB-18835-E

PAGE 42
Yard, Chicago, Illinois, 1955
Photograph by Ken Hedrich,
Hedrich-Blessing, courtesy Chicago
Historical Society, HB-18109-G

PAGE 43
*Log house, Knott County,
Kentucky, 1930*
Photograph by L.J. Peet, National
Archives

PAGE 44
Two picket styles
The Stewart Iron Works Company,
Covington, Ky.

SELECTED BIBLIOGRAPHY

Allport, Susan. *Sermons in Stone: Stone Walls of New England and New York.* New York: W. W. Norton & Co., 1990.

American Society of Planning Officials, Planning Advisory Service. *Fences.* Information Report 113. Chicago: American Society of Planning Officials, 1958.

Ashley, Burton M. "Old Cape Cod Fence-Posts." *Landscape Architecture* 13 (October 1922): 19-26.

Bourcier, Paul G. "In Excellent Order: A Gentleman Farmer Views His Fences, 1790-1860." *Agricultural History* 58 (1984): 546-64.

Brown, R. Ben. "The Southern Range: A Study in Nineteenth Century Law and Society." Ph.D. diss., University of Michigan, 1993.

Brown, Robert Harold. "Snow Fences: Then and Now." *Journal of Cultural Geography* 4 (1983): 87-98.

Bugliari, Joseph B. and Dale Arrison Grossman. *Fences: New York Law.* Ithaca, N.Y.: Department of Agricultural Economics, New York State College of Agriculture and Life Sciences, 1988.

Centre National de la Récherche Scientifique. *Les bocages: histoire, écologie, économie: aspects physiques, biologiques et humains des écosystèmes bocagers des régions tempérées humides.* Rennes, France: I.N.R.A./E.N.S.A./Université de Rennes, 1976.

Cronon, William. "World of Fields and Fences." In *Changes in the Land,* 127-56. N.Y.: Hill and Wang, 1983.

Danhof, Clarence H. "Fencing Problem in the Eighteen-Fifties." *Agricultural History* 18 (1944): 168-86.

Dick, Everett. "Fences." In *Conquering the Great American Desert: Nebraska,* 70-92. Lincoln: Nebraska State Historical Society, 1975.

Dole, Philip. *Picket Fence in Oregon: An American Vernacular Comes West.* Eugene: University of Oregon, School of Architecture, 1986.

Drago, Harry Sinclair. *Great Range Wars: Violence on the Grasslands.* N.Y.: Dodd, Mead & Co., 1970.

Evans, E. Raymond. "Palen Fence: Example of Appalachian Folk Culture." *Tennessee Anthropologist* 3 (Spring 1978): 93-99.

Fife, Austin E. "Jack Fences of the Intermountain West." In *Folklore International,* D.K. Wilgus, ed., 51-54. Hatboro, Pa.: Folklore Associates, Inc., 1967.

Flynn, Charles L. "The Privileges of Property." In *White Land, Black Labor: Caste and Class in Late Nineteenth-Century Georgia,* 115-149. Baton Rouge: Louisiana State Universtiy Press, 1983.

Gard, Wayne. "Fence Cutters." *Southwestern Historical Quarterly* 51/1 (1947): 1-15.

Geerlings, Gerald K. *Wrought Iron in Architecture.* New York: Charles Scribner's Sons, 1929.

Giese, Henry. *Farm Fence Handbook.* Chicago: Agricultural Extension Bureau, Republic Steel Corp., 1938.

Groth, Paul. "Lot, Yard, and Garden: American Distinctions." *Landscape* 30/3 (1990): 29-35.

Hahn, Steve. *Roots of Southern Populism: Yeoman Farmers and the Transformation of the Georgia Upcountry, 1850-1890.* N.Y.: Oxford University Press, 1983.

Harper, Roland M. "Some Interesting Statistics of Fences." In G. Ward Hubbs, "Fencing: A Note." *Alabama Review* 37 (1984): 221-26.

Harris, Marshall. *Origin of the Land Tenure System in the United States.* Ames: Iowa State College Press, 1953.

Hart, John Fraser. "Field Patterns in Indiana." *Geographical Review* 58 (1968): 450-71.

Hayter, Earl W. "Barbed Wire Fencing—A Prairie Invention: Its Rise and Influence in the Western States." *Agricultural History* 13 (1939): 10-20.

Hayter, Earl W. "Fencing of Western Railways." *Agricultural History* 19 (1945): 163-67.

Hayter, Earl W. "Iowa Farmers' Protective Association: Barbed Wire Patent Protest Movement." *Iowa Journal of History and Politics* 37 (1939): 331-62.

Hayter, Earl W. "Livestock-Fencing Conflicts in Rural America." *Agricultural History* 37 (1963): 10-20.

Hayter, Earl W. et al. "Free Range and Fencing." *Heritage of Kansas* 4/3 (1960).

Herman, Bernard L. *The Stolen House.* Charlottesville: University Press of Virginia, 1992.

Hewes, Leslie. "Early Fencing on the Western Margin of the Prairie." *Annals of the Association of American Geographers* 71 (1981): 499-526.

Hewes, Leslie and Christian L. Jung. "Early Fencing on the Middle Western Prairie." *Annals of the Association of American Geographers* 71 (1981): 177-201.

Holt, R.D. "Introduction of Barbed Wire into Texas and the Fence Cutting War." *West Texas Historical Association Year Book* 6 (1930): 65-79.

Hunter, J. Marvin, Sr. "Convicted for Fence-Cutting." *Frontier Times* 28 (Oct. 1950): 20-22.

Jackson, John B. "Public Landscape." In *Landscapes and Selected Writings of J.B. Jackson,* Ervin H. Zube, ed., 153-60. Amherst: University of Massachusetts Press, 1970.

James, Jesse S. *Early United States Barbed Wire Patents.* Maywood, Ca.: By the author, 1966.

Johnson, Hildegard Binder. *Order Upon the Land: The U.S. Rectangular Survey of the Upper Mississippi Country.* N.Y.: Oxford University Press, 1976.

Jordan, Terry G. and Matti Kaups. *Backwoods Frontier: An Ethnic and Ecological Interpretation.* Baltimore: John Hopkins University Press, 1989.

Kantor, Shawn Everett. "Razorbacks, Ticky Cows, and the Closing of the Georgia Open Range: The Dynamics of Institutional Change Uncovered." *Journal of Economic History* 51 (1991): 861-86.

Keystone Steel & Wire Co. *Keystone Steel & Wire Co., 1889-1989: A Centennial Celebration.* Peoria, Ill.: Keystone Steel & Wire Co., 1989.

Kilpinen, Jon T. "Traditional Fence Types of Western North America." *Transactions of Pioneer America Society* 7 (1992): 15-22.

King, J. Crawford. "The Closing of the Southern Range: An Exploratory Study." *Journal of Southern History* 48 (1982): 53-70.

Leechman, Douglas. "Good Fences Make Good Neighbors." *Canadian Geographical Journal* 47 (1953): 218-35.

Linden-Ward, Blanche. "'Fencing Mania': The Rise and Fall of Nineteenth-Century Funerary Enclosures," *Markers* 7 (1990): 34-58.

Long, Amos Jr. "Fences in Rural Pennsylvania." *Pennsylvania Folklife* 12/2 (1961): 30-35.

Lyman, F. A. "Economic and Engineering Problems in Farm Fencing." *Agricultural Engineering* 11 (1930): 329-32.

Lyman, F. A. "Farm Fencing Needs Economic Engineering Study." *Agricultural Engineering* 10 (1929): 317-320.

Martin, George A. *Fences, Gates, and Bridges: A Practical Manual.* N.Y.: O. Judd, 1887, 1909; reprint, Brattleboro, Vt.: Alan C. Hood & Co., 1992.

Mather, Eugene Cotton and John Fraser Hart. "Fences and Farms," *Geographical Review* 44 (1954): 201-23.

McCallum, Henry D. and Frances T. *Wire That Fenced the West.* Norman: University of Oklahoma Press, 1965.

McClure, C. Boone. "History of Manufacture of Barbed Wire." *Panhandle-Plains Historical Review* 31 (1958): 1-114.

McFadden, Joseph M. "Monopoly in Barbed Wire: The Formation of the American Steel and Wire Company." *Business History Review* 52 (1978): 465-489.

Meaker, G. L. and L.C. Bailey. "History of the Manufacture of Barbed Wire." Typescript, 1913. American Steel and Wire Company Collection, Baker Library, Harvard University.

Meaker, G. L. and L.C. Bailey. "History of the Manufacture of Poultry Netting and Meshed Fabric." Typescript, 1913. American Steel and Wire Company Collection, Baker Library, Harvard University.

Meaker, G. L. and L.C. Bailey. "History of the Manufacture of Woven Wire Fencing." Typescript, 1913. American Steel and Wire Company Collection, Baker Library, Harvard University.

Meredith, Mamie. "The Importance of Fences to the American Pioneer." *Nebraska History* 32 (1951): 94-107.

Meredith, Mamie. "Nomenclature of American Pioneer Fences." *Southern Folklife Quarterly* 15 (June 1951): 109-51.

Murray-Wooley, Carolyn and Karl B. Raitz. *Rock Fences of the Bluegrass.* Lexington: University Press of Kentucky, 1992.

Nickl, Peter, ed. *Zäune, Gitter, Tore.* Munich: Bayerischer Handwerkstag e.V., 1986.

Noble, Allen G. "Fences, Walls, and Hedges." In *Wood Brick and Stone: North American Settlement Landscape.* Vol. 2, *Barns and Farm Structures*, 118-33. Amherst: University of Massachusetts Press, 1984.

Noble, Allen G. and Jean M. Danis "Literature on Fences, Walls, and Hedges as Cultural Landscape Features." *Pennsylvania Folklife* 33/1 (1983): 41-47.

Norris, Darrell A. "Ontario Fences and the American Scene." *American Review of Canadian Studies* 12/2 (1982): 37-50.

Padgitt, James D. "Mrs. Mabel Day and the Fence Cutters." *West Texas Historical Association Yearbook* 26 (1950): 51-67.

Patrick, Vanessa E. "Partitioning the Landscape: The Fence in Eighteenth Century Virginia." Microfiche. Colonial Williamsburg Foundation, Department of Architectural Research, 1983.

Peters, Alvin. "Posts and Palings, Posts and Planks." *Kansas History* 12 (1989-90): 222-31.

Primack, Martin L. "Farm Fencing in the Nineteenth Century." *Journal of Economic History* 29 (1969): 287-91.

Portland Cement Association. *Concrete Fence Posts.* Chicago: Portland Cement Association, 1917.

Poulsen, Richard C. "Hawks and Coyotes on Western Fences: Symbolism of Slaughter." In *Pure Experience of Order*, 56-69. Albuquerque: University of New Mexico Press, 1982.

Powell, Edward P. *Hedges: Windbreaks, Shelter, and Live Fences: A Treatise on the Planting, Growth and Management of Hedge Plants for Country and Suburban Homes.* New York: Orange Judd Co. 1900.

Rafferty, Milton D. "Limestone Fenceposts of the Smokey Hill Region of Kansas." *Pioneer America* 6 (1974): 40-45.

Randall, Kathleen. "Early Wire Fences." *Old House Journal* 20 (March 1992): 28-31.

Raup, H.F. "Fence in the Cultural Landscape." *Western Folklore* 6 (1947): 1-12.

Reaburn, Pauline and Ronald. "Fence Patterns on Old Canadian Farms." *Canadian Geographical Journal* 95 (1977): 36-41.

Reynolds, Arthur R. "Land Frauds and Illegal Fencing in Western Nebraska." *Agricultural History* 23 (1949): 173-79.

Rice, Mary Louise. "Role of Osage Orange Hedge in the Occupation of the Great Plains." M.A. Thesis, University of Illinois, Urbana, 1937.

Richards, W.M. "Fencing the Prairies." *Heritage of Kansas* 4/2 (1960). Rikoon, J. Sanford. "Traditional Fence Patterns in Owyhee County, Idaho." *Transactions of Pioneer America Society* 7 (1984): 59-69.

Rose, Ramsey. "Chain Link Fences: Definition of Space and Sense of Place in the American Urban Landscape." *MASS: Journal of School of Architecture and Planning* 6 (University of New Mexico, Fall 1988): 21-23.

Scott, William B. *In Pursuit of Happiness: American Conceptions of Property from the Seventeenth to the Twentieth Century.* Bloomington: Indiana University Press, 1977.

Savage, William W. "Barbed Wire and Bureaucracy: Formation of the Cherokee Strip Live Stock Association." *Journal of the West* 7 (1968): 405-414.

Shaklee, Ronald V. "Barrier Use and Urban Territoriality." Ph.D. diss., University of Kansas, 1983.

Southworth, Susan and Michael. *Ornamental Ironwork: An Illustrated Guide to Its Design, History and Use in American Architecture.* Boston: David R. Godine, 1978.

Stilgoe, John R. *Common Landscape of America 1580-1845.* New Haven: Yale University Press, 1982.

Symons, Harry. *Fences.* Toronto: McGraw-Hill Ryerson, 1958.

Taylor, Albert D. "Notes on Construction of Ha-Ha Walls." *Landscape Architecture* 20 (1930): 221-224.

Taylor, Lonn. "Rails, Rocks, Pickets: Traditional Farmstead Fencing in Texas." In *Built in Texas*, ed. Francis Edward Abernethy, 177-91, Waco, Texas: E-Heart Press, 1979.

Temple, Wayne C. "Lincoln's Fence Rails." *Journal of Illinois State Historical Society* (1954): 20-34.

Truitt, Esther Ruth. "Enclosing a World." *Utah Historical Quarterly* 56 (1988): 352-59.

Tyler, Ransom H. *A Treatise on the Law of Boundaries and Fences.* Albany: William Gould and Son, 1874.

United States Department of Agriculture. Bulletins. Humphrey, H.N. *Cost of Fencing Farms in the North Central States* (1916). Kelley, M.A.R. *Farm Fences* (1940).

Molander, Edward Gordeon. *Farm Fences.* Bulletin (1954). *Farm Fences* (1961). Timmons, Merril S. Jr. *Fences for the Farm and Rural Home* (1971).

United States Department of Agriculture. "Laws Relating to Fences and Farm Stock." In *Report of the Commissioner of Agriculture for the Year 1869*, 394-410. Washington: Government Printing Office, 1870.

United States Department of Agriculture. [Horace Capron], "Statistics of Fences in the United States." In *Report of the Commissioner of Agriculture for the Year 1871*, 497-512. Washington: Government Printing Office, 1872.

Upton, Dell and John M. Vlach. *Common Places: Readings in American Vernacular Architecture.* Athens: University of Georgia Press, 1986.

Vernon, Arthur. *Estate Fences: Their Choice, Construction and Cost.* London: E. & F.N. Spon; N.Y.: Spon & Chamberlain, 1889.

Wafios Maschinenfabrik. *Energy + Flexibility: 75 Years Wafios Maschinenfabrik Reutlingen.* Reutlingen, Germany: Wafios Maschinenfabrik, 1968.

Washburn & Moen Manufacturing Company. *Fence Laws: Statute Prescriptions as to the Legal Fence.* Worcester, Mass.: Washburn & Moen, 1880.

Washburn & Moen Manufacturing Company. *The Fence Problem in the United States, as Related to General Husbandry and Sheep Raising.* Worcester, Mass.: Washburn & Moen, 1882.

Washburn & Moen Manufacturing Company. *Fence Question in Southern States.* Worcester, Mass.: Washburn & Moen, 1881.

Webb, Walter Prescott. *Great Frontier.* Austin: University of Texas Press, 1964, 1986.

Webb, Walter Prescott. *Great Plains.* Boston: Ginn and Co., 1931, 1959.

Wheeler, David L. "Texas Panhandle Drift Fences." *Panhandle-Plains Historical Review* 55 (1982): 25-35.

White, William R. "Illegal Fencing on the Colorado Range." *Colorado Magazine* 52 (1975): 93-113.

Williams, Michael. *Americans and Their Forests: A Historical Geography.* Cambridge: Cambridge University Press, 1989.

Winberry, John J. "The Osage Orange, A Botanical Artifact." *Pioneer America* 11 (1979): 134-41.

Withers, Robert Steele. "Stake and Rider Fence." *Missouri Historical Review* 44 (April 1950): 225-31.

Zelinksy, Wilbur. "Walls and Fences." *Landscape* 8/3 (1959): 14-20.